RAGS *to* RICHES
to the

Real Me

HEATHER Walton

RAGS *to* RICHES
to the

Real Me

Overcoming Adversity Through
a Lifelong Quest for
Success and Happiness

by

HEATHER WALTON

The *Real Me* Limited

MEDICAL WAIVER

The author of this book is not dispensing medical advice or prescribing the use of any technique as a solution for physical, emotional, or medical problems. Please seek the advice of a physician or other qualified healthcare professional for any medical or psychological situation. The author intends to offer general information and skill-building techniques to help you in your quest for emotional and spiritual wellbeing. If you use any of the information in this book, neither the author nor the publisher assumes responsibility for your actions. THE USE OR RELIANCE OF ANY INFORMATION CONTAINED IN THIS BOOK IS SOLELY AT THE READER'S RISK.

Pressure makes diamonds.[1]

---

1 George S. Patton, Jr., https://www.goodreads.com/quotes/53033-pressure-makes diamonds

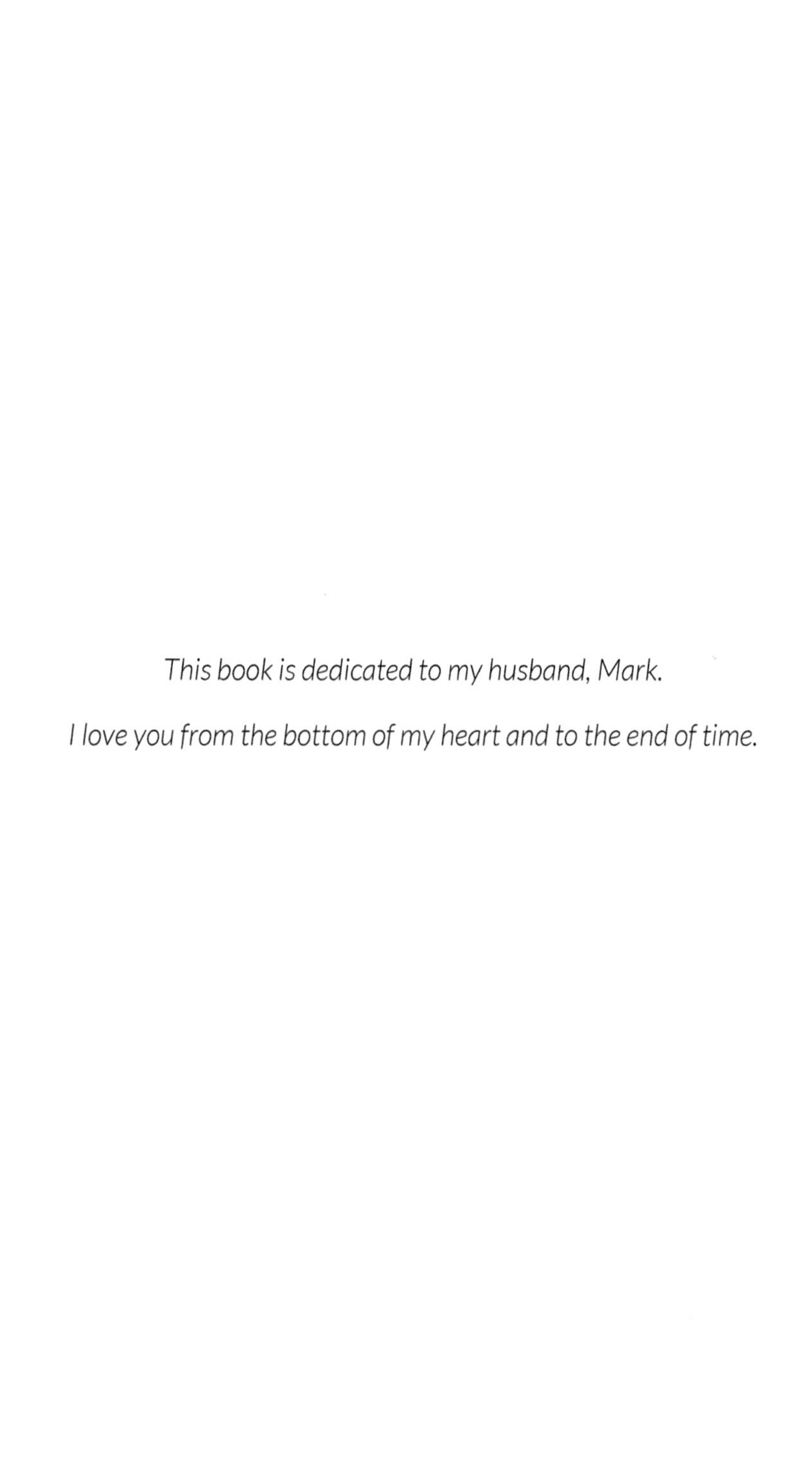

This book is dedicated to my husband, Mark.

I love you from the bottom of my heart and to the end of time.

Contents

Foreword

When I first met Heather Walton, a tall, slim, gorgeous blonde in designer clothing, she was already a self-made success who exuded confidence and energy. Heather had won every award achievable in her chosen industry. To this day, she is a successful multi-office business owner. Little did I know of Heather's background. Before me stood a successful young woman supported by a loving husband. Awe inspiring, yet at the same time intimidating, Heather epitomized success. But how did she achieve it?

The quote "Never judge a book by its cover" may sound cliché, but as Heather takes us on a very personal real-life journey, you'll discover it could not be more apt. From humble beginnings, through life's highs and lows, trials and tribulations, sheer grit and determination, Heather shows us that anything is possible.

Everyone can achieve greatness no matter what life throws at you.

When you engage with these pages you will be engaging with Heather Walton in a raw and relatable way through real life experiences that have helped mold and shape the person she is today, while also discovering her own self-worth and success. Her valuable life lessons and easy-to-implement self-help tips will assist you in overcoming any shape or form of adversity. You will feel her genuine desire to help you learn, grow, and be the best version of you.

Adversity can be turned into an advantage. Rock bottom is merely a springboard. Let Heather's experiences guide you in reaching new heights.

Treena Drinnan AREINZ

Auckland, NZ 2022

I believe in the right place, and the right time. Although I always knew I had a book to write, I was never sure when I'd find the time to write it. It feels like I fell asleep and woke up—and there it was. I have a gift for channeling words and I feel it's my life's purpose to write words that uplift, inspire, and serve others. I don't expect this book will be for everyone (you can't please all people all the time, but you can please some of the people some of the time). I try with all my heart to please all people all the time and feel disappointed when I don't. I guess I just like to see the best in people. I'm not perfect. I forgive others' downfalls, knowing they're not perfect, either. No one is.

I recall that once, when I was five, a girl snapped at me for patting her dog. I was shocked. From that moment on, I was disappointed with people and always wondered—*Why do people hurt other people?* Still, I kept patting dogs—thousands of them—and never had that reaction again. That taught me to never, ever give up. Sometimes, stuff just happens.

I've lived a full, challenging, amazing life. If the story of my life's journey can benefit someone, or provide enjoyment or help to someone, then this book has been a success. Thank you for reading it. I wish you every success on your path from Rags to Riches.

Acknowledgments

want to thank...

... my mum, who taught me how to be tough on the outside and soft in the center—like she was. Even while she fought lung cancer (and lived for twelve more years with one lung), she barely complained. All she wanted was my time. Showing love and affection wasn't Mom's strong point, but there wasn't a moment that I doubted how much she loved me and would sacrifice for me. I know how immensely proud of me she was—and will be to see this book published.

... my dad, for being my best friend growing up. I hope you and Mom are now flirting and being kids again in heaven. I know how much you loved her.

... my son, for giving my life purpose. Thank you for allowing me to write about our life, and for giving me a reason for living in those early dark days. I love you.

… the friends who have stayed by my side—you know who you are. I haven't been the easiest person to love and have been on such a crusade for the last fifteen years, I haven't had a lot of time to put into our friendships. But when I need you, you're there—so thank you.

… my stepdaughters, Grace and Bella. Thank you for letting me be your "Smum." You have filled a gap of not having a daughter myself. Having you both in my life is a blessing. I just love being a young Grandma to our wee Hazel. She is the apple of our eyes.

… Melissa Ambrosini, thank you for your mentoring, for inspiring me to get started, for giving me the initial structure for the book, and for giving me faith that I could do this. Your talent inspires me.

… Anoushka Van Rijn, thank you for coming to my rescue with all your gorgeous energy and enthusiasm. Your love and support of empowering women is uplifting and you made the styling of the front cover such a fun experience for me. I just love what has been produced. Thank you.

… Ella Kiliuyi, your loyalty, love, support and friendship means everything to me and I feel blessed every day for having you in my life. All your work in the background in every area of my life means I was able to get this book written and out to the world. Without you this would not have been possible.

… Treena Drinnan, thank you for being the first to read the book and giving me the confidence to keep going and get it out to the world to read.

… Michael Ireland, my awesome editor. Thank you for giving me the confidence that I had written something worth reading, and for organizing it in a professional, readable way. I couldn't have done this without you, that's for sure. Thanks to the Universe, for showing me the path to find Michael!

… Rachel De Leon, thank you for stepping up and contributing your amazing proofreading skills to the editorial team.

… Maira and Kristin, I could not have done this without you. You have been the absolute icing on the cake and have made this last part of getting the book out to the world both fun and inspirational. Thanks to you both, I feel like writing another one so we can do it all over again. True professionals.

… Mark, for loving me no matter what life throws at us or what I threw at you. Thank you for your inspiration, for giving my life such purpose, and for being the reason I want to be a better person every day.

… my readers, thank you for reading this book. Many blessings on the journey ahead.

Heather Walton

Introduction

The Crazy Thing About Money

The thing about money is that if you are flat broke and miserable, someone else in the same situation could be deliriously happy. Some of the happiest people I've ever met were living in India and had nothing, but they were beautiful, grateful human beings living their best life. Money wasn't something they desired—they wanted peace and happiness. Helping others was their deepest passion and they were living their truth.

How many people do you know who are super wealthy but miserable? If you think money will buy you happiness ... sure, it may make you happy for a while. It may give you choices you wouldn't have had otherwise, but it won't be a magic potion for true happiness in every sense of the word. It's probably just a small part of your happiness equation—the rest of your happiness comes from other sources, and together all those things make up a healthy, balanced pie graph that represents your happiness.

I know firsthand that money doesn't bring happiness, because my first experience with wealth brought me utter unhappiness. My life began with me wearing rags—well, hand-me-downs and homemade clothing—to attaining riches beyond my wildest dreams. I ran away from every penny and everything attached to that life and started over, just to let go of the misery it created.

In this book, I take you on a journey of how I manifested wealth—at a massive cost to my mental health and physical well-being—and then let it all go and manifested it again with a happy outcome. I learned that being rich or poor doesn't equal happiness or misery—because you can be happy or miserable in either situation. The goal, of course, is to have the wonderful material things you want and deserve in your life, while also having the beautiful, soulful happiness that fulfils you and makes your heart sing.

There are all kinds of beliefs out there about money and happiness. Make no mistake, you can have both. It may have taken me a few laps around the "Rags to Riches" block to get it right, but I did. Now that I have both money and happiness, I'm not letting them go. Hell, no!

I wrote this book because I want to share my story with you, in the hope that you can learn how to acquire wealth and happiness, create your own Truth, and live your best life, just like I did.

The Crazy Thing About Life

The crazy thing about life is that everything happens at the perfect time and in the perfect place, giving us the perfect lessons we need. Once you realize this, you'll feel a tremendous sense of relief. You'll be able to sleep better at night, knowing that nothing bad can happen to you—and that if something bad happens, it's for your greater good. So, you don't have to worry because all will be well soon.

I can hear some of you going, "Yeah, yeah." But it's true—this is your life's journey. Sometimes you don't have a choice about how things pan out, but you can choose how you react. You can choose to rise above it all. Life can serve up some real challenges that have you questioning everything. Believe me, I know. But don't let it define you. Use every experience you have to springboard you toward something better.

In my experience, if you cannot acknowledge the bad things that happen to you, and if you cannot thank the universe for the teachings it brings you (or at least accept them), you will continue to receive those messages (i.e., you will continue to be sent stronger and stronger messages) until you listen, make changes, and move forward. Once you listen, messages will materialize because you'll be looking for the signs. It's like buying a yellow car and thinking it's unique, but suddenly you see yellow cars everywhere. Why? Because you are now open to yellow cars.

We've all heard stories about beautiful people who seem to have awful things happen to them repeatedly. Sadly, it's the universe trying desperately to make them listen, trying to guide them toward making changes in their lives. I know that's a hard pill to swallow. Bad things happen to great people. But how many times have you had something terrible happen to you and later, when you recount what took place, you say things like, "But if it hadn't happened, I would never have met my gorgeous husband," or "If it hadn't happened, I would never have gotten this great new job or appreciate the great family I have," and so on.

As you read this book, I encourage you to keep a journal, and take notes or write down the tips and actions that resonate with you. Since you are reading this book, my bet is that you have had similar experiences in your life. So, I provide tips I hope you will consider—because I think they'll help you turn your own rags into riches—whether figuratively or literally! I also include some "Real Me Actions" for you to undertake, which will cement in your mind changes you wish to make to improve your life or deal with past trauma. I believe that emotional and physical trauma, whether minor or major, needs to be brought into the light to be healed and released, not left in the shadows where it creates fear. Let's work together as I bring my shadows into the light—and help you do the same.

Rags to Riches Tip – Consider the Flip Side

Can you think of times in your life when you asked, "Why did this happen to me?" "What did I do to deserve this?"

Grab your journal. Draw a vertical line down the center of a page. See if you can find three moments in your life when you asked these questions. Write them down in the left-hand column. Then, in the right-hand column, write down the flip side of each—the positive things that arose as a consequence. You'll feel a real sense of achievement. You'll realize that you listened to the lesson the universe gave you and you turned it into a positive. Try it right now—look for that lesson.

What Happened to You? What Was the Lesson You Learned?

Believe and you will achieve. If you can have blind faith that the universe is there to help you achieve your greatest good and to give you what you need in perfect, divine timing, then it will be so. You'll know it's not possible to get it wrong. It's all just another beautiful lesson sent from the stars, especially for you, for your beautiful divine soul. I love the saying: "Everything works out in the end. If it hasn't worked out yet, then it isn't the end."[2]

---

2 "Tracy McMillan Quotes," Brainy Quotes, accessed July 10, 2022, https://www.brainyquote.com/authors/tracy-mcmillan quotes.

Are you ready to make some changes to your life? Great, get your journal and favorite pen ready, so you can make notes as you read, and so you'll be able to complete the Rags to Riches exercises sprinkled through this book.

Here is my story...

Chapter One:

Growing Up in Ramarama

Becoming Heather

My life's journey has taken me from Rags to Riches—twice. But in order to help you understand how I started out as a country bumpkin living on the "wrong side of the tracks" in Ramarama, New Zealand, and ended up in an upper-class beachside home in an affluent neighborhood, I have to start my story at the beginning.

I began life as a shy child, with no self-esteem, no sense of belonging, and an enormous challenge for a little kid: panic attacks. My earliest memory of a having a panic attack was at age five. I was staying at my friend Larissa's house and I was excited—

it was my first sleepover. I'd met Larissa at primary school and she was my first best friend. I felt grown up going to school and was delighted to have connected with this lovely girl.

Larissa's house was beautiful compared to ours. I felt privileged that she wanted to be my friend! We lived on the main road that went through our small, rural town. I walked home from school every day along the asphalt road. It had no footpath, and was bordered by rough metal—I had to walk along the stone edge that often sloped down into a ditch. When I arrived at our driveway, the rough metal extended all the way to our house.

Larissa lived across the road, in a large, beautiful brick home with a concrete driveway, not a rough gravel/metal drive like ours. They even had a solid wooden gate across their driveway. We never had a gate. Our house was called a Keith Hay home, which was built in a factory and shipped in one piece on the back of a truck onto our land. Larissa's house was a design-built home on a perfect, meticulously laid foundation. Their house was built brick by brick into a lovely, one-level sprawling home with outdoor walkways that led to the paddocks where they kept their horses. Having my own pony was such a dream! I saw their big house daily and I watched her ponies wandering around the perfect post-and-rail paddock. She had several ponies, including a little white Shetland, who was like a miniature horse, just large enough for us to ride.

Larissa's big horse was a Bay mare. I had the best time playing and having fun with Larissa and her horses—I just loved their smell and I especially loved that big brown mare. I felt like a princess living a dream. I remember once we were sitting backward on the horses, doing our homework on their big backsides. We giggled as the horses walked around the enclosure, and all our pens and paper ended up on the ground. As the light grew dim, we brushed the ponies off, put their covers on, and let them go into their paddocks for the night.

After we made our way inside their beautiful home for dinner, I started feeling nauseous. The busyness of the afternoon had swept me away—I'd been so carefree. But once inside, I missed Mom. I started having catastrophic thoughts: *What if mom and dad get abducted by aliens while I'm here? What if when I go home everyone is gone?* I felt so many emotions bubbling up. As I looked around the designer kitchen and lovely interior-designed home, I felt sad for my parents, who lived in such a humble, tiny little house. Our entire house would have fit into Larissa's living room. But they were my mom and dad and I loved them. I couldn't eat my dinner that night. Food was the last thing my body wanted; it was on the verge of a fight-or-flight reaction. Uncontrollable, catastrophic thoughts kept washing over me, like waves crashing onto rocks. My tummy did flips. I felt sick and had to run to the bathroom. My body just purged.

By bedtime, I was crying; inconsolable. I was confused. *What's going on?* I didn't know what to do. I wanted to go home. Larissa's dad took me home—he walked me across the road. I was so embarrassed, I never stayed at their house again. I learned it was okay to play in the afternoon but not to stay the night. I became exceptional at making excuses that "I can't, I have to go home."

Of course, I didn't know I was having a panic attack. Instead, I labeled it "homesickness." But when I became an adult, I realized I'd been having panic attacks since that fragile young age. Those were also my earliest memories of feeling unworthy and "not good enough." *Why would Larissa want to be friends with me? Her house is beautiful. We don't even have a concrete driveway, it's more like a mud path. My brother even had to carry me to the car once when I was dressed up to go out, so I didn't get my shoes muddy.*

When Mom and Dad bought their land, there was an ancient bungalow at the back of the property. They told us they would demolish it and build a new house, so we were allowed to write all over our wallpaper. A good seven years later, our brand-new, tiny three-bedroom, one-bathroom house was plonked on the ten-acre block and we moved in. Our first Christmas in the new house was so exciting! The power and water weren't connected; it was like camping.

No one ever finished the base of the house. We could see through the floorboards to the foundations. Years later, it was just the same. It was a plain, weatherboard, cheaply built 70's house, with yellow carpet and textured wallpaper. The kitchen bench was orange Formica, and the cupboard doors were brown. We had a round, top-loading dishwasher. The bathroom vanity was tiny; it had a plastic basin and plastic bath. The steps to the front door were a death trap—they were just dropped at the door and were never aligned with the door frame. You took your life into your hands every time you walked on them, and when it was raining it was next-level dangerous. There was no landscaping, no driveway. Most of the property felt temporary; there was a growing list of things to do or to fix when and if we had time or money. In twenty-plus years, that list never got touched, and the house remained frozen in time—both my parents gave up on the property. It amazes me now—six people lived in that wee house.

I shared a bedroom with my sister, eighteen months older than me. As the youngest of four kids (three girls and a boy), by the time the hand-me-down clothes got to me, they were, well ... mediocre and well-worn. The alternative to wearing them was to make my own. I remember receiving a lemon-colored dress with elastic shirring through the bodice, little shoestring straps, and a long skirt. I liked it, because I wore it for one of my school photos. Another outfit that makes me cringe looking back, was a pinafore Mom made for me out of a tartan fabric. It looked like a bad patchwork quilt, but I didn't mind it because she had made it for me and it was new. I had school photos taken in that dress too, with a little turtleneck sweater underneath.

In high school, we learned to sew. We learned how to make a sweatshirt, and I made about five of them; they cycled around our family for years. My sisters were talented at sewing—one of them made my dress for the school ball. It was cheap white satin fabric—I loved it. It wasn't quite finished by the time the ball came around, though, so the boning in the bodice stabbed me all night. I felt so spoiled, I had a new pair of shoes (even though they were from the No. 1 Shoe Warehouse). They were white to match my dress, and they had a little white button on the side-strap. The heels were high for me, and being tall, I wobbled around in them. Still, my sisters had done my makeup and my hair was up ... I felt fancy. Early in the evening, one heel broke on those nasty shoes. I felt like Cinderella, limping around. It was embarrassing for this self-conscious teenager; I couldn't wait to leave. Later in life, I was a stepmom to five beautiful teenage girls at different times—three with my first husband and another two with my current husband, Mark. I ensured their school ball experience was the polar opposite of mine. They had their hair and makeup done by professional stylists and makeup artists and dressmakers tailor-made beautiful gowns for them. They arrived in limousines and danced until dawn.

Our ten-acre block was mortgaged to the eyeballs. Mom and Dad had greenhouses on our property, in which they grew tomatoes. We sold tomatoes for twenty cents a kilo at the market or at our roadside stall. We would pile into the old, rusty blue Bedford truck—it had round headlights and the cab at the back was an enormous square box we stacked high with boxes. There were double doors we could open right up or shut tight and bolt closed. Sometimes it was fun to ride in the back. Over its lifetime, that truck had various people attempt to bog up the rust, so it was patchy all over.

So, we'd all pile into the truck and head over the hills to Pukekohe and sell the tomatoes at the Turners and Growers yard. I used to love running around the concrete produce yards, picking up stray potatoes and onions that fell out—I'd fold up the bottom of my skirt and make it into a carry bag, collect the stray vegetables, and ferry them back to the Bedford truck and take them home to Mom.

I loved going with Dad to the market. He'd say, "There's no point in you coming, Heather, you'll just fall asleep."

"No, no. I won't. I promise," I'd say.

Dad's truck had the gears on the steering column, and I remember watching him shifting gears. As we'd get going, I'd just about bounce off the front seat thanks to the ancient suspension. The gauges on the old-fashioned dashboard would flicker as we set off along the road, bouncing up and down. The loud humming of the engine, the bouncing of the seat, and cuddling up to Dad would soon send me off to sleep as we wound our way around the Bombay Hills on the way to the produce yard. Happened every time.

One time, I was in such a hurry to dive into the front seat with Dad, I yanked on the big old passenger door, lurching my whole body to close it behind me, and slammed my finger in the door. The shriek I let out got poor Mom running to my rescue. Poor Mom—living on our junky old farm, there were plenty of traps for Mom and her busy tribe of kids. A week wouldn't go by without someone falling through a pane of glass in the greenhouse, falling off something or standing on a nail from the old ruin of a bungalow that stood, semi-demolished, at the back of the property for most of my adolescence.

But most of the time, the trip to Pukekohe vegetable yards was uneventful. Sliding across the big leather bench seat, I'd get as close to Dad as I could. He'd be wearing his grubby old jeans and smelled of tomatoes and dirt. To this day, I can't smell a tomato without thinking of Dad.

Keeping the hundreds of tomato plants in the greenhouses flourishing was hard labor—my poor parents always seemed to be shattered. Mom seemed to be disappointed with her lot in life. Dad was a frustrated inventor—he made an eight-bucket trolley out of iron rings, into which buckets fit. We'd roll the trolley through the greenhouses. We could pick eight buckets of tomatoes before returning it to the shed to pour them into a clever grading machine he also invented. The tomatoes traveled up a little conveyer belt made of rollers covered in carpet. The belt got progressively smaller and smaller in width, and as the tomatoes rolled along, we graded them into various sizes. We sat at the end of the belt holding boxes, and when we pressed a pedal with our foot, a little trap door opened, and the tomatoes rolled into cardboard boxes. When a box was full, we released the pedal and the little trap door closed, retaining the tomatoes. We placed the boxes on a rolling, manual conveyer belt on which they made their way to the end of the shed and into the old Bedford truck. It was fun working in the sheds.

Mom used to reminisce about her days as a beautiful young nurse and she'd tell stories about what she and her friends got up to in the nursing home where they all worked. I learned more about Mom when she passed away, and when I wrote her obituary, than I ever knew about her when she was living. I learned how much she loved her youth with her girlfriends, being footloose and fancy-free. After they'd finish their nursing shift, they'd put on dresses they had sewn themselves and go out and dance the night away. Mom loved us kids but I felt like she had sacrificed so much of herself. She wasn't fulfilled or happy most of her life. She never put herself first—and her bitterness and disappointment were obvious.

From a young age, my sisters Lucy and Jojo chose different paths than our parents did—heading straight to the Light and the spiritual path of enlightenment. We all sought it out and ran toward it. It's not that Mom wasn't spiritual, in fact, our seeking of the Light made her do so as well. When Jojo was running a retreat in Majorca, for example, she paid to fly Mom over to cook at the retreat.

Cooking was a genuine passion for Mom. One of my fondest memories is of Mom's amazing cooking and the delights she cooked up for her four hungry kids. We were all so happy that Mom got to travel and do something that was a genuine passion for her. She had little of that during her life.

Rags to Riches Tip – Create Your Bucket List

- *Are you afraid you will get to the end of your life without fulfilling your dreams?*
- *What's on your bucket list?*
- *Grab your journal and write down ten things you want to do in this lifetime and have still yet to do.*
- *Try to put a timeframe on when you will tick those things off your To-Do list.*

My story of being homesick is one of many rinse-and-repeat (i.e., it happened over and over) stories of my childhood. From an early age, I was disappointed with human beings. There is a photo of me at about age three cuddling two little dogs at the local calf-club day, a fun day at primary school, when the kids got to take their pet lambs or calves to the school and compete for prizes. As I cuddled the little dogs, a mean girl ran straight up to me and right into my face, she snapped, "Those are not your dogs. They are mine!" She grabbed them and took off. I was shocked and confused—all I was doing was giving love to the dogs—*Why was she so mean?* From that day onwards, I was cautious and on guard around people. The loving little girl I once was changed: I became conditional, and great at pushing people away, being horrible to them so they wouldn't want to be my friend. *What if they find out*

I'm just a poor little girl living in a muddy Keith Hay farmhouse with six people sharing one bathroom? It terrified me.

As a pretty little blonde girl, I felt like an imposter. I didn't belong in this life. After a while, a lifelong pattern emerged: Anyone who got close to me got their head bitten off, so I could dump them before they dumped me.

As with most young girls, at about age thirteen, my body changed. One day, I was staring at myself in the mirror, looking at my pancake chest. They had teased me at school for having a flat chest—the boys called me an "ironing board." They say that if a boy teases you, it's because he likes you, but that was not the way I saw it. Being an "ironing board" buried me further in my lack of self-worth. As I studied every inch of my body, I realized, *I'm lopsided.* Around my waist, one side differed from the other—*I'm crooked!* I dressed and ran to find my mother. "Mum, look at this," I said. I lifted my shirt so she could see my waist. As a nurse, I knew Mom would know what was going on with my body.

"Hmmmm," she said. "Think we better see the doctor."

The doctor did X-rays. I had to take a train into the city to see a specialist. I went on my own, a brave little thirteen-year-old, X-rays under my arm. It was a big deal to go alone into the city, let alone deal with the news the specialist delivered to me with no one there to support me.

"You have two scoliosis in your spine," the specialist told me. "The lower one is thirty degrees and the top one is thirty-three degrees. In fact, you're lucky you have two because if you had one, you would lean over to one side."

That was it—I had a crooked spine. Nothing could be done. I felt ugly, disfigured. It scared me to wear togs or a bikini in case anyone noticed how crooked I was. Not the greatest for a vulnerable thirteen-year-old with body consciousness issues.

Rags to Riches Tip – Build Your Belief Systems

- *What were your teenage body issues and beliefs?*
- *Do you think they were valid? Were they made up? Or were they a result of someone being mean to you?*
- *Do you still feel you have those issues? How did you resolve them?*
- *Close your eyes and sink into your body. Scan your body in your mind, starting at the top of your head. Moving slowly, visualize each part of your body in your mind's eye. Are there areas you cringe at or feel uncomfortable about? Now say to yourself, "I love and appreciate my legs/tummy/arms (for example). Say it even if you don't believe it or it doesn't sit well with you. We only have one body and every part of us needs love and appreciation. Have you ever heard someone say, "I hate my back?" or "I hate my stomach?" Imagine how the poor back or stomach feel. Often those parts of the body give up and increase their pain to attract attention from you. I believe negative talk to your body can cause "dis-ease." So, practice self-love and give your body the love and gratitude it*

deserves. It needs to carry you around for a very long time so it's time to love the skin you're in.

It was good that I understood little about my body. I wasn't in pain and being ignorant about what would happen later in life was bliss. I was an anxious young lady, and the stress my body was under, put pressure on my nervous system, further activating my panic attacks and anxiety. I wasn't aware of any of this.

When I was thirteen, my sisters were sixteen and twenty, and they had been doing a rinse-and-repeat cycle of their own. They influenced me, sharing things they were listening to and reading. Somehow or other, I discovered the writer John Kehoe. I wanted money and to have a better life—I think that's what led me to him. His book, *Money, Success & You,*[3] got me thinking about wanting more for my life. I learned about positive affirmations and the power of positive thinking. The best part was you didn't even have to believe the affirmations or positive thoughts in order to achieve them. You just had to be super clear about what you wanted, write your list, read it every day, and achieve. As an

[3] John Kehoe, *Money, Success, and You* (Montreal: Zoetic Inc., 1998), https://www.amazon.com/Money-Success-You-Harness-Prosperity/dp/0969755155.

imposter, telling myself that I was beautiful, worthy, healthy, wealthy, and wise just made me think, *Like yeah, right*. But things changed in my life. I manifested great things faster and faster. I was on the right path.

Rags to Riches Tip – Decide on Five Things You Want

- *What are five things you want for yourself, even if you have no belief that having them is possible? The world is your oyster. Write them down.*

- *You may want to own a superyacht—seriously. Later in the book, you'll read that I end up owning a 105-foot superyacht, so I'm not kidding. Reach for the stars! What do you REALLY, REALLY want? It's just like in the Spice Girls song, "Wannabe"[4] ... just say what it is you want.*

- *Make yourself a dream board. Hang it up on your wall in a conspicuous place and look at it every day. If you live in a small space and don't have an empty wall you can tack a dream board on, create a goals list instead. Keep it in an accessible place, like at the front of your journal, and pull it out daily. Add dreams and goals to it as your dreams grow and change. (In this book, we'll refer to dream boards and goals lists. Goals are usually relating to feelings and desires or wants. A goal is something you want to achieve. A dream, on the other hand, is usually something you want to buy or*

---

4 Spice Girls, "Wannabe," recorded December 1995, track 1 on *Spice*, Virgin, 1996, compact disc, https://www.amazon.com/Greatest-Hits-Picture-Disc/dp/B07QMB53C6.

manifest. So, a goal is to be happy; a dream is to buy a boat. Creating a dream board or a goals list, or both, is an easy way to keep track of what you want so you can stay focused and achieve your goals and dreams!)

Just about every self-help book you'll ever read and every motivational speaker you'll ever listen to will tell you to do the same thing: set goals. Here's what's fascinating: It's easy to write goals, but ninety-five percent of people who write their goals down fail to do the step that sinks in and seals the deal. They don't *read their goals every day.*

If you are a visual person, make yourself a dream board. Hang it up on your wall in a conspicuous place and look at it every day. This is a cool exercise to do as a family—because the entire family (or you and your partner) are all putting collective energy into achieving these wonderful goals. It helps you manifest them a lot faster. Hang your dream board on the fridge, on your mirror, or in a place you look at daily.

One thing I manifested when I was young was a modeling career. Could I achieve it, even with my twisted little body? It was almost like I had to tick that box. As a young soul, I was looking for validation that I was worthy. For me, like many girls, modeling seemed to be the pinnacle of success and acceptance. During the school holidays, I worked at a local café and saved enough money to book into a course run by the famous modeling agency owner and mentor, Doreen Morrison. I adored her. She was a glamorous older woman, always dressed beautifully, with make-up and hair perfect—and she smelled incredible.

There were many little successes on my short modeling journey. Being accepted to the course was big for me—I felt like a winner just being in Doreen's class. Doreen made me feel special. I'm sure she did that with all the girls, but I felt exceptional. She had a sense of people and loved genuine, nice people; she was not interested in the bratty, self-centered girls. She loved girls who were kind and caring, saying that their internal beauty shone on the outside. Because I was tall and skinny, she said I'd be perfect for the runway. I trembled with excitement as we practiced prancing up and down the runway. I'll always be grateful to Doreen for her "Lessons from the Catwalk"—teaching me that standing tall (even if you are a little crooked), putting a smile on your face (no matter how you feel inside), and getting out there (whether or not you feel like it), is always the best way forward. "Fake it until you make it," she used to say ... "Or believe and you will achieve." It's a winning strategy I've applied to my whole life— thank you, Doreen!

Chapter Two

Creating Dream Boards

Getting Specific

have so many examples of how the goals list and dream board work in action. One of my best "getting specific" stories is about the "shopping list" I wrote when I was looking for my beautiful husband, Mark. This took place after my first round of rags-to-riches—I was back at rags, and I was broke. Heart broke, soul broke ... broke in every sense of the word. I was a single mom. I had no money, no hope, nothing. It was a bleak road. Even writing this now, my heart breaks a little when I think of my desperately sad situation.

I was with my beautiful friend Justine, who was in a similar situation (minus a few of the nasty things that had happened in my life), but we were both single and sad. We were enjoying one of our last evenings together in my enormous home (before the house went to its new owner and I was out on the street), and I said to Justine, "Damn it, we deserve better than this. Get a piece of paper. I know how to do this stuff. We're going to conjure up the perfect man. Grab your witch's hat, let's make up a brew."

We laughed.

"No holding back," I told her. "Let's get specific, girlfriend." So, we dove in, silent, scribbling, each of us making a list of what we wanted in a man. I still have my list:

- Must be taller than me.
- Must drive a nice car.
- Walks into a room with confidence.
- Is confident and self-assured.
- Is funny and makes me laugh.
- Must love my little boy like he was his own.
- Has a great job he enjoys.
- Loves every square inch of me.
- Builds me up, doesn't bring me down.
- Knows what he wants in life.
- Accepts me for who I am.
- Is open to spirituality and my beliefs.
- Supports me in my endeavors.

We finished our lists, shared them with each other, and giggled. Within three months, we had met our Marks. Yep, they were both called Mark. Justine is married to her Mark and has two beautiful little girls. I married my Mark and I thank the universe every day for sending him to us. My son James and I gained a best friend, and he is our rock. The cherry on the top is I also got two beautiful new daughters, and as I'm writing this, I'm now a grandma, which is an absolute delight. Bonus!

It wasn't all roses though for Mark and I, from day one, and entering into a relationship with children from other marriages certainly had its challenges. But finding my perfect man was certainly the right place to start.

Rags to Riches Tip – Write Your List – Let's Keep a Journal

If you are single or in a relationship that is not serving you, write your list. Keep a daily journal and read your list every day. The romance angels will get to work and start shaping your path and your life to lead Cupid to your door. The lovely thing about doing this is that your current relationship can also benefit—and you may fall in love with your partner all over again.

If your relationship ends because of this exercise, then just know that the universe has sent your partner away and the romance angels are going to work to find the partner for you that serves you at this time in your life.

Manifesting and Dream Boards

I got everything on my list, including Mark being open to spirituality and my beliefs. We were both at a similar stage in our lives—he too had left a marriage that no longer served him and, being the great man he is, he set his ex-wife up with her own home so their children would suffer as little disruption as possible. He left the marriage with very little and, just like me, faced restarting all over again. My heart went out to this beautiful man. Like me, he had worked weekends for as long as he could remember to set his family up, only to walk away from it all. The exhaustion on his face was obvious. We were two broken people, but together we made a whole—and off we went, supporting each other and creating our dream life together.

We created a joint dream board on the computer with pictures of all the beautiful things we wanted to achieve. It had double the power when we both looked at it daily. After fourteen years, we are masters at this, and we have limitless beliefs about what is possible for us. Our dreams and aspirations now differ vastly from what they were when we met. Back then, we knew we needed to manifest as fast as we could so we could get the most precious commodity of all: *time*.

It's the most satisfying thing in the world to pull out your goals list or dream board and tick off the items you've manifested. When we were looking for a home, for example, we stood in a house we wanted to buy and said, "Oh my goodness, it's the same house we put on our dream board. Very white and clean, with a large blue swimming pool!" We purchased a similar house and put the pool in ourselves. Looking back at the dream board, we realized we had, in fact, manifested our version of that house.

I'm not kidding about reaching for the stars. Mark and I struggle to think of things that are wildly beyond our dreams now because we have achieved most of the financial goals we ever set out to attain—and there aren't too many material things left we could want. Now our goals are more around our family, our time together, and what we can give to others—and that's both exciting and satisfying for us.

Can you believe it? The title of this book—*From Rags to Riches*—is exactly what happened in my life! I know, 100 percent, that anything is possible for anyone—and this means you. If you have passion in your belly and follow the simple tips in this book, you can manifest anything and everything you could want. There are some rules and guidelines, however, and we'll get into those shortly.

One question I get asked a lot is, "But Heather, what if my dream board isn't working?" My answer always is, "Well, look for where the blocks are—and it's not always you." For example, during my second rise to riches, I was the number one salesperson in New Zealand within the Ray White Real Estate group. I was selling up a storm. But every once in a while, for no real reason, a house just would not sell. At that point I'd analyze the owner-family and ask myself, "Which one isn't letting go?" Often, it was a child, manifesting as hard as he or she could for the house not to sell. Children can be the most powerful manifesters on the planet. So, if a child or a family member dug in and was pulling huge amounts of "bugger off" energy to the house, no one would buy it and there was nothing anyone could do to change that. Sometimes, if the family found a new home, then little Johnny or Judy would get excited about the new pool in the new house, and he or she would drop the negative energy, the house would sell, and up went the "Sold" sticker. Phew! It's always a much quicker sale if the whole family is on the same page!

Rags to Riches Tip − Put on the Brakes

Like the family in the example above, do you recall a time when you put the brakes on something that you and your partner were at odds about wanting or creating? Did it work? How did you resolve this?

When you are a couple or a family, it's powerful to share or create a dream board together to make sure that you are all on the same page. For example, there is no point in one of you trying to manifest a concrete home when your partner wants a weatherboard home. Work together on your joint goals list or dream board and have a collective focus on what you want to manifest for yourselves as a couple or a family. It's okay to have your own personal goals and couple or family goals.

You and your family manifest all kinds of things into your life, both positive and negative, every day. Once you realize this is happening and you have an OMG moment, you'll realize, "Jeepers, I better get some structure around this—otherwise, it's a runaway train." Yep. Whatever you want you will get, and whatever you focus on that you don't want you will also get. You must stay conscious about the conversations in your head. It's time to tune in, people, and start manifesting magic, not madness. One of my husband's favorite sayings is "This is not a dress rehearsal, people, this is life. Start living your best one now." It's true. In order to manifest what you want, you've got to stay positive, and stay focused. Focus on the negative, and you'll manifest the negative.

I see this in action daily. For example, one of my golf buddies has a lot of negative self-talk. Recently, she lined up to take a shot, saying "What do you bet I hit the tree?" Yep, she hit the tree. She was so focused on not hitting the tree, she hit the tree. Her entire golf game goes that way. "I don't want to go in the bunker," she says ... and she goes in the bunker ... and so on. I wonder, if she had said with as much confidence and relaxation, "Hey watch this, I'm going to get a hole in one," whether she might get a hole in one. Negative self-talk will manifest just as fast as positive self-talk. So, watch what you say, flip your thoughts to a positive, and watch your world change.

As I noted earlier, I'm sharing my life-changing journey with you hoping you can both learn from my mistakes (without making them yourself!) and take advantage of the Eureka! moments I had that transformed my life in so many good ways. The timeline of my story jumps around a little, however, so just know that the tale is not linear. But don't worry, because every step along the path I walked is packed full of teachings you can apply to your own life. So, stay with me—and hang on for the ride.

Chapter Three:

Setting My Dreams in Motion

Walking the Path from There to Here (Going Backward to Move Forward)

So, how did I go from being a sad little country bumpkin to being a successful businesswoman? To explain the path I took, I need to take you back to my childhood again.

Our family home was in a small rural area about ten kilometers (6.2 miles) from the nearest town. Our little primary school went up to intermediate grades, but my mom sent us to intermediate school in town so we'd get used to a bigger school before the enormous step to college. (Our local college had a pretty good name back then, but these days, it's one of the worst areas in Auckland, and you'd do everything you could not to send your child there.)

At school, I did as little as possible in order to pass. It's sad looking back—I was so bright, but I never thought it possible that I'd go to university, so there didn't seem to be any point in striving to pass the university entrance exams. Looking back, I wonder if Mom and Dad realized they didn't encourage us, or perhaps they just knew they wouldn't be able to support us financially. By the time I came along as child number four, they were exhausted and just couldn't be bothered. So, as I saw it, I had two choices: Do nothing and become nothing or motivate myself and be everything I could be with the resources available. I chose the latter.

I know I wasn't an easy child (and was quite a wild child). Maybe that's why my parents gave up trying to parent me. If Mom said "black," I'd say "white." My sisters used to call me "a fart in a bottle." I was often exploding with energy, bursting forth willy-nilly, and leaving destructive shards behind me, unaware of the carnage I left in my wake. I think an element of that still exists within me. But I was independent early in life—I thought I knew everything. I was always on a mission to get to the finish line, tick the box, and move on to the next thing. At fourteen, I was driving a car—a year before legal driving age. I still had low self-esteem at that point, and my rinse-and-repeat cycle was to hang out with an unsavory crowd—kids I felt were well below me. It made me feel better; I wasn't embarrassed about bringing them home and letting them see where we lived.

When I was a teenager, my older siblings left the nest—as quickly as possible—and entered the work force, became independent, and lived on their own, away from home. It was exciting for me to visit my sisters. They had set up pretty little nests, so much nicer than the home we were raised in. I couldn't wait to leave home and create a space I could be proud to have visitors enjoy. The upside of being the only child left at home was that I had my own room. I made it into my sanctuary, decorating it with plants, nice bed linen, and whatever I could find. I even invited the odd friend around to hang out in my room. We'd make a beeline for my room, pass the adults by, and hang out in my haven, my bit of pride.

By this point, I was immersing myself in self-help books … branching out of John Kehoe into the likes of Anthony Robbins[5] and Louise Hay.[6] Mom had joined a network marketing cosmetic company (to manifest money without having to slave in a hot greenhouse, picking tomatoes all day long while my father snoozed on the sofa complaining of a sore back). The company provided Mom with many motivational tapes to listen to, so I

---

[5] Anthony Robbins, *Unleash the Power Within* (New York: Simon & Schuster, 2020), https://www.amazon.com/Unleash-Power-Within-Personal-Transform/dp/1797111612.

[6] Louise Hay, *You Can Heal Your Life* (Carlsbad, CA: Hay House Inc., 1984), https://www.amazon.com/Heal-Your-Companion-House-Lifestyles/dp/156170878X.

borrowed those and listened to Zig Ziglar[7] and others.

I wrote and read my goals daily. I meditated and said affirmations. I learned them off by heart, and I walked around, telling myself positive things all day long. My favorite go-to affirmation, a catch-all sentence (that I still say to myself today) is below.

Rags to Riches Tip – Get Better Every Day in Every Way

"Every day, in every way, my life gets better and better."[8] … "I am healthy, wealthy, and wise." Sometimes I vary the last bit—which I did to manifest a little more kindness into my spoken word: "Every day, in every way, my life gets better and better. I love and accept myself unconditionally and my spoken word is one of love and kindness to others."

Create a little card of positive affirmations about the size of a business card. Laminate it and keep it in your pocket. When you slip your hand into your pocket, it will trigger you to run some affirmations through your head and top up your positive vibes for the day. If you go down a negative train-of-thought rabbit hole, reach into your pocket, touch the card, and snap out of it.

---

[7] Zig Ziglar, *How to Be a Winner* (Wheeling, IL: Nightingale Conant Corp., 1990), https://www.amazon.com/How-Be-Winner-Zig-Ziglar/dp/1555253830.

[8] "Émile Coué > Quotes," Goodreads, July 16, 2022, https://www.goodreads.com/author/quotes/192066._mile_Cou_.

When I was doing these affirmations, if a negative thought entered my head, I would stop it and change my thoughts to a positive. It became a natural part of my life. Another cool little reset tool I learned was that if my day was going a bit pear-shaped, I would pause, head to the bathroom, shut the cubicle door, and do this exercise.

Real Me Action — Visualizing White Light

Close your eyes. Breathe out. Imagine a bolt of white light heading down from the universe. Imagine there is a little lid at the top of your head—this is your Crown chakra. Open that lid and let the white light of the universe pour into your head and down into your body. Imagine cork plugs popping out of the ends of your fingers and toes and the white light bursting all the way through you, down your arms, out through your fingertips and out the tips of your toes, taking any negativity or dark energy with it down into Mother Earth.

Next, visualize that you are sitting cross-legged inside a pyramid. Pop your corks back into your fingertips and toes as the white light continues to fill up your body. Feel the white light flowing down the outside of your body, filling the pyramid up to the apex. Shut the lid at the top of your head, enclosing the white light inside your body, and then seal your triangle, encasing yourself in a pyramid of white light. Thank the universe and open your eyes.

You are bullet proof. Bring it on.

If you want to set yourself up for a loving day with a solid foundation of love and light, head to my website, download this meditation, and listen to it every morning. You will attract less conflict, any discord that does come your way will flow away, your spoken words will be soft, and others will listen to you and savor your positive energy.[9]

I have used this daily ritual for years and still do. These days it's a re-energizer for me and an old habit, but back then, I needed to use it to make myself strong enough to face the world when I was at my most fragile. After I did the ritual, harsh words just slid off me and I handled difficult things a lot better. This meditation keeps me grounded and protected from other people's agendas and bad energy.

This ritual is amazing at bringing people into your energetic sphere. Years ago, when I was in a spiritual circle in London (UK), we did what we called a "head merge." This is where you partner

---

[9] Heather Walton, "Heather Walton," The Real Me Limited, August 4, 2022. https://www.theheatherwalton.com.

up with someone, press your foreheads together, and allow your third eyes to interact—then you tell the other person what you saw. The person I merged with said, "I see you sitting cross-legged, in a meditative position, at the base of a pyramid. This is your foundation, your protection." Wow! I was blown away. Talk about a positive reinforcement validation moment.

You will get better and better at this. These days, I can do this exercise in thirty seconds or fewer. I can shut my eyes anywhere, re-center, rinse off the negativity and then go back into the world, recharged. It's a great exercise to do right before you have an interview or do some public speaking—or you can use it to prepare for any stressful situation you find yourself in.

Rags to Riches Tip – Acknowledge Your Achievements

An important part of your journey should be acknowledging your achievements. If you don't thank the universe and pat yourself on the back, why would you get anything else ever again?

What can you acknowledge and be grateful for that you have overlooked in the past? Is there something you loved achieving but you don't recall ever having acknowledged that you did, in fact, create it—and that you achieved something you worked for? We often move on quickly from our achievements—before we savor them.

Take out your journal and start a list of all the things you've achieved. You may wish to start off small and then move to list the larger things. Often in life, things start off small, and then suddenly, we have achieved great things. But because they happen over time, we take them for granted without acknowledging what an amazing milestone or achievement we've accomplished.

Think back through your life and write a timeline of major events. You will realize how much you've accomplished. Pat yourself on the back now. Express your gratitude for having achieved so much.

Embracing Change and Asking for What You Want

So, as a teenager, armed with my new lessons and rituals, I began to change. My life improved. I left school after the fifth form (which is now year twelve). I was impatient to be an adult—I wanted to get into the driver's seat of my life, drive my own vehicle, and get out there. Back then, my goals seemed huge, insurmountable. Now, looking back, I see that they were tiny. But for me, it was baby steps forward, and each one seemed like a significant achievement.

My first job after leaving school and entering the adult employment world was working in a joinery company as an office administrator. I had no training, but I did my best. My job was to go through (what seemed like thousands of) invoices from supply companies and code them to the correct job. It was almost impossible, as most of the trades didn't provide the supplier with the job address. So, it was a guessing game. It was a male-dominated company, and back then, sexual harassment was alive and well. As a pretty little blonde, that job didn't last long. One day, my boss was super rude to me and swore at me. My dad stepped up and told my boss where to go. And that was that—the end of my first experience in the workforce. Hmmmm, ouch. Not great for the self-esteem. But I'd been doing a lot of self-development work, so at least I didn't plummet into the depths of worthlessness again. I brushed it off, and thanked the universe for the experience and for helping me get clear on what I wanted to do rather than what I didn't want to do.

Rags to Riches Tip – Thank the Universe

A handy little tip when you find yourself in a situation you don't wish to be in is to thank the universe for the opportunity ... tell it that it's not quite right, and say, "What I really want is...."

Thank you very much for my________________, but it doesn't have the _________________ I really want. What I really want is _________________.

In my situation I said, "Thank you, universe, for my first job. But it wasn't the supportive, friendly environment I was hoping for. What I really want is a lovely boss who is friendly and supportive and trains me."

Treat it like an incorrect shopping order. "Oh, thank you so much. But this wasn't quite what I ordered."

It's the same for a relationship that doesn't quite fit.

Getting the Perfect Job

Next, I got a job in a second-hand furniture shop. I learned I was an exceptional salesperson. I enjoyed that job. I was working for an older couple, Mike and Faith, who had made plenty of money in their lives, but they had bought a business and wanted to do something different, enjoyable, and less stressful. Mike and I would head out in his big old truck to people's houses, he would give them a price for their goods, then we would load up the truck and head back to the shop to unload the furniture, clean it up, and price it. Mike was such a sweetie to work for. He spoke to me with respect and treated me like an adult, happily teaching me the job and giving me life lessons as we went along. Mike and Faith trusted me so much they could go away on holiday and leave me in charge. That job was everything I had asked the universe for.

I earned enough money to rent a little villa nearby and boy, did I deck it out. It was stunning. Any furniture that came in that I loved, Mike would let me buy cheaply, and soon I had a home that I *loved*, filled with gorgeous antiques and collectables. I had a gold velvet sofa and a glass and brass coffee table with matching shelves I put all my house plants on. I had pretty wall mirrors, a Persian rug, a solid oak bedroom suite with a headboard, and a sweet antique dining room table with matching chairs. I was bursting with pride and couldn't wait to have friends and family come and visit me. It was wonderful to feel like this for the first time in my life.

Even though I loved my job, my home, and my new life, my self-esteem and self-worth were still low. And, while my boyfriend at the time was a hundred times better than my previous boyfriends had been, he was still not a patch on what I really wanted or what fulfilled me emotionally or spiritually. I wanted to feel attracted to my man. I wanted to be spoiled. I wanted someone to buy me flowers and treat me like a princess.

I let him go with love and took what I thought was a step up—I connected with another young man who had many fine qualities. My new guy, Michael, had been a friend of my sister for years and was a lot older than me. I'd always thought he was gorgeous, so I was pretty proud when I caught his eye. He was so talented—he sang in a band and played drums and harmonica, and he was brilliant at drawing. I would get home from work and he'd have spent the day drawing a cartoon in intricate detail. He had played for quite a famous all-girl band in Australia and toured most of

New Zealand. I couldn't believe how he could play the drums, harmonica, and sing, all the while keeping perfect time. He had the most beautiful long curly blond hair and he reminded me a lot of Robert Plant back in the day. We had a beautiful little kitten we named Fleetwood, and one day, I got home and he had spent the day making a movie about Fleetwood. This was his way of spoiling me.

Spending time with a band and having a boyfriend who was the center of attention was a real challenge. I had to dig deep to feel secure. On New Year's eves, girls flocked onto the stage and threw themselves at the band for New Year's Eve kisses. Jeepers, I had to suck it up when that happened!

Michael's parents were delightful, and I loved feeling like part of a bigger family. Their house was gorgeous, they drove beautiful cars, went on delightful holidays, and for all intents and purposes, they were a normal, functional family—something I'd always wanted. Their support kept our relationship strong—for more years than it would otherwise have lasted.

I was still house proud, and Michael and I had set up a beautiful home. We had lovely things, and we enjoyed having people over and entertaining them. We felt proud of our little pad. Michael was passionate about his music, and I admired him for living a life true to what made him happy.

Michael had restored a gorgeous little Mark One Ford Cortina. One day, after a gig, I was getting ready to drive it home, with his beautiful Rogers drum kit in the back. He leaned in the window and said, "Drive carefully. Everything I love in the entire world is in this car." What an angel. He was everything I wanted at that time in my life. For seven amazing years, me and my muso-man had a lovely relationship. I toured NZ with his band, dancing and playing the groupie. But attending gigs every weekend and having a Monday to Friday stay-at-home boyfriend didn't fit with my now-ambitious outlook on life. So, one day I said, "I love you so much, Michael, but I need to leave you. If I stay, I will want you to change." I let him go with love and let him carry on being a wonderful musician and enjoying his vintage car and drum kit. I hope he found a love who loved him the way he was.

Rags to Riches Tip – Set It Free

As author Richard Bach said in his book, Jonathan Livingston Seagull, "If you love something, set it free; if it comes back, it's yours. If it doesn't, it never was."[10]

What is something you had to let go of because you knew that ultimately, it would not work for you in the long term? This might have been a habit, a person, or a partner.

---

10 Richard Bach, *Jonathan Livingston Seagull* (New York: Scribner, 2006), https://www.amazon.com/Jonathan-Livingston-Seagull-Richard-Bach/dp/0743278909.

Making Compromises – Fake It 'Till You Make It

When I was a little girl, I fantasized about being a lawyer (but never put any thought into how I would achieve this without going to university). I had always thought that helping the underdog was a fantastic thing to do. Whilst avoiding people with money at school, I always stuck up for the kids that got picked on in class. I remember, for example, sticking up for a boy called George, a short, tubby kid with thick glasses and a posh British accent. He used to wrinkle up his nose when he talked. Boy, did I try to save that boy over and over. I found out later in life that George had committed suicide. It is sad that human beings find others' weaknesses and love to press their buttons to inflict pain on them.

So, I was passionate about standing up for weaker people and for what I believed in. I always felt most like my authentic self when I was doing this. Of course, I couldn't afford to go to university and study law, so while I was working at the furniture shop, a job came up at the local district court, and I jumped at it. A friend of mine worked at an employment agency. She helped me get the interview, and long story short, I landed the job! Being the smart cookie I was, I grasped the role easily, and my confidence and self-esteem grew. Soon, I was sitting proudly on the bench next to the judge, running the court as madam registrar. My parents were so proud.

Being a registrar of a district court in a low socio-economic area had its challenges. One of my jobs was to run deposition hearings. This was when a stenographer would type up evidence as it was being given, and before the witness was let go, I would read their evidence back to them, and they would sign it, confirming that it was correct, and the judge would admit it as evidence. I read evidence relating to anything from burglary to violent rape. Sometimes, reading evidence was disturbing. It was hard to switch off at night, go home, and sleep soundly when that day I had read about a criminal who had premeditated a break-in, then had broken into a home and raped the poor lady who lived there. I was paranoid to the max. I was still meditating and manifesting positivity, but just as quickly, it was being flushed out of me at work. My method and daily ritual were to rush to the bathroom after each court case, center myself, and "rinse off" the negative people and scenarios I was coming across all day, every day.

I switched from criminal court to family court, thinking it would be less confrontational—only to find that family court was all about the bad treatment of children and listening to their parents fight over them (all with little or no regard for these poor kids' sanity and well-being). One day, the judge and I were given the heads up that a father who had lost custody of his son was on his way to the courtroom to kill the judge. We were locked in the courtroom and had to stay put until the police apprehended him. The emotions of these people ran high when it came to children and loved ones. This was heartbreak in its toughest form.

My dad knew I was disappointed that I'd never been able to qualify as a solicitor, so he paid for me to do a legal executive course, which I studied part-time while working in the courts. In my role, we had a lot to do with the local lawyers in the courtroom. We would chat and catch up with each other before court was in session and we all got to know each other well—it was the best part of the job. My lawyer friends knew I had completed my legal executive diploma and to my delight, a local law firm shoulder-tapped me and offered me a role in resource management—a hundred miles from yucky criminal or family court law. Woo hoo and wow! How far the little, unqualified blonde girl from Ramarama had come!

So, once again, I sent my job back to the universe saying, "Thank you so much. I love my legal job at the courthouse, but I don't want to work in the crime or the family division." The universe had presented me with another job that suited what I wanted and that was much better for my well-being. For the next two years, I worked as an executive assistant for a law firm partner who was the local district council solicitor. I enjoyed the job; I learned about local body rules and regulations. We looked after the council when the public was challenging them or if they were trying to proceed with a local community project to which the public objected. The partner I worked with was a tough boss who had a long history of EAs not working for him for long—and I was no exception.

I looked for another job, farther afield from my hometown. I was super keen to branch out of the area I had grown up in, and to get away from memories and people. I applied for many legal executive jobs. I was a cute twenty-four-year-old with long legs. My skirts were always short, not because I wanted them to be, but because my legs were so long, an ordinary-length skirt was short on me. I landed the most amazing job in a fancy boutique property law firm. The furniture was gorgeous. My jaw dropped when I walked into the office, like *Wow!* It was the start of a twelve-year journey—I had landed on my feet. I had made it.

The job itself, however, was way beyond my capabilities. It was in property law, which I hadn't had experience in. I was amazed I'd even got the job. But I knew that if I worked hard, I could learn on the job and be worthy of the role. I had to fake it to make it. Many years later, when I was one of the most valuable employees in the company, my boss told me he had only employed me because I wore a short skirt and that it was a real bonus when I turned out to be an amazing legal executive. Go figure. This didn't matter to me—I was earning substantial money, loved my job, and it had taken me out of my little hometown. It was a clean start for me

Of all the things I had done, I was most proud of this job. I became an important member of the firm, and after ten years, I sat in on board meetings and partners' meetings, and the team valued my input. I was paid well (more than most of the young lawyers), and I got to a point where, even if I had gone to university and gotten a Bachelor of Laws (LLB), I wouldn't have been earning what I was, and I wouldn't have had the respect I had earned in the firm. I had made it—the universe didn't care that I didn't have a law degree. All the manifestations, affirmations, and hard work I had put in had come to fruition. The universe had looked at my shopping list of what I wanted and it had delivered. This was a big moment of realization for me. I had the money, the respect, and the job satisfaction of any solicitor—all without an LLB! I felt amazing. My sense of worthiness and self-esteem were high.

Chapter Four:

Wanting More for My Life

Believing in Myself

The fruits of my affirmations, visualizations, manifestations, and meditations were unfolding positively, and things moved fast. I was ticking goals off my list, and my self-esteem and confidence were growing. I started believing I could do anything and achieve anything. To challenge myself on a personal level—I felt I couldn't do any better professionally—I widened my thoughts about what I wanted to do. Remember the little girl with the panic attacks? I wanted to take her by the hand, help her deal with her phobias, and leave them behind once and for all.

Deep in my belly, I still had a fear of staying anywhere overnight. The home sickness I felt was terrifying and hadn't dulled since I was that little girl at Larissa's house. At that point, even the thought of traveling somewhere made me nauseous. I'd hyperventilate, and I couldn't breathe. You and I both know that this is what it feels like to have a panic attack. *Why is this happening?* I'd wonder.

One explanation was that it might have been an original trigger related to my big brother, John. Ten years older than me, John was a big, burly, annoying fifteen-year-old whose favorite pastime was torturing his five-year-old sister. Don't get me wrong, John has a heart of gold and he's devastated that his rough playfulness caused me a lifelong issue. I was a typical irritating little sister, and with no television in our house, we were always looking for ways to amuse ourselves. When John wasn't out shooting things, he was irritating me.

John was on the spectrum (and was probably an undiagnosed ADHD). But he was just like any other teenager—pushing boundaries, testing relationships, and so on. The trouble was, our exhausted parents couldn't be bothered most of the time to deal with his behavior. John had always been "on the go." When he was tiny, if Mom wasn't watching him, he'd disappear. One time, she found him a mile up the road, watching a digger in a paddock. Another time, she lost him in town, only to find him balancing precariously on a mile-high pile of shoe boxes in a shoe shop—he'd climbed a ladder and scrambled up the boxes. Mom was never one to panic, and as the entire shop freaked out, Mom talked John down.

My mom had four miscarriages before she gave birth to John. He was the most wanted little person. Born with the umbilical cord wrapped around his neck, he almost didn't make it. He was small and a little malnourished, so he didn't get the greatest start in life. John was disappointed when Mom and Dad added our sisters to their brood, thinking in his little mind, "Why am I not enough? Why do you need another baby?" Still, he loved his sisters. Later in life, he proved this when he and my two sisters all ended up in the UK at the same time on different journeys. John told me he always had enough money in the bank to send the girls' home if they ever needed to go. The truth was, they earned five times more than him and were self-sufficient, but that's just John.

When we were little, John played tricks on me. I'd wail, and Dad would fly into a rage. Dad didn't want to deal with the fallout of a screaming toddler because her brother was mean to her. So, he'd punish John the only way he knew how—a clip around the ears, a belt on his behind, and worse sometimes. I felt guilty that my brother got a hiding because of me, and I'd slink off to my room and cry, feeling awful, hating myself for causing my brother pain. My poor brother.

I remember annoying John, too. One day, he said, "Right, I'll sort you out." He grabbed a huge blanket, wrapped me up, and sat on me. I couldn't breathe. I was terrified. My mind went wild. I thought I was going to die. Every catastrophic thought ran through my mind. John ignored my screams and cries, and laughed for what seemed to me like hours. Maybe it was only thirty seconds, but that utter loss of control damaged me for life.

From that day onwards, I became a control freak. I was claustrophobic. I wouldn't go in an elevator. The thought of being in a car, plane, or on public transport, where I couldn't just hop off when I wanted to, terrified me. I didn't get on a plane until I was twenty-four years old—and even then, panic and anxiety would come over me. First, I'd tremble, then shake, and then the nausea would start. When the body goes into fight-or-flight mode, it stops functions it doesn't need so it can focus on running—so it was common for me to run to the bathroom and either vomit or have diarrhea. Charming.

But I forgave John and overcame my phobias by forcing myself to do things that scared me—like flying and scuba diving. I read a book called *Feel the Fear and Do It Anyway*.[11] It became a bit of a mantra in my head when faced with anything that made the anxiety rise in my stomach.

Rags to Riches Tip – Let It Go

Has anything like this ever happened to you? Perhaps as a child? Was there ever a situation that affects you to this day? I'm not one for dredging up old hurts and fears, but sometimes it helps

---

[11] Susan Jeffers, *Feel the Fear and Do It Anyway* (New York: Ballantine Books, 2006), https://www.amazon.com/Feel-Fear-Do-Anyway/dp/0345487427.

to acknowledge it and let it go.

- *What issues, fears, and old hurts do you continue to "go to" and blame your feelings on?*
- *Do you attach blame to those events?*
- *Who is to blame? Or what is to blame?*
- *Let's resolve them once and for all.*
- *I forgive ________________________ for ________________________. When I think of this person/situation, I feel ________________________*

  ____

  ____

  ________________________.

- *But this no longer serves me, so I let it go with love and move on with my life, grateful for this life lesson in forgiveness and surrender."*

Facing My Fears

Enrolling in a scuba diving course was one of the most challenging, scary things I could think of putting myself through to combat my claustrophobia. Plus, my job was all rock, no roll. I had great job satisfaction, and it was time to push boundaries in other ways. I had become so confident; I didn't want to let my panic attacks define me or stop me from experiencing life to the fullest. My sister Lucy did the diving course and introduced me to her dive instructor, Paul. He was super cute, and I wanted to get to know him. I wanted to enroll in his course and see if I could overcome the fear I had of boats and scuba diving. If I got to know him and trust him, I decided, it could help me grab this challenge and overcome a massive fear. What an achievement that would be! So, I enrolled in the course, knowing it would be an immense challenge. Could be worse … cute dive instructor. Paul was part Fijian; my friends called him a bronzed god. My self-esteem had grown to a point where I thought, "I deserve to date someone this gorgeous. I'm going for it. This could be a win-win situation, dating someone handsome while overcoming some ingrained fears."

Paul was amazing, and I adored him. He lived in the city, and with my new legal job also in the city, we moved into a flat together close to my work. He was a fitness freak, so we used to run together, go to the gym together, and, of course, scuba dive together. He was a big family man, so once again I got to inherit a gorgeous family who, while they were very emotional people, they were a loving, supportive, tight-knit family. Island families are so close and I fell in love with them all, cousins and grandparents, aunties and uncles.

Paul's friends were as outgoing as he was and I loved them, too. Weekends were spent with him teaching classes and taking people out on dive trips, which I went on, too. My panic attacks and claustrophobia were still there, but I had become familiar with them and, most of the time, I acknowledged them, experienced them, and let them go ... "Oh here comes that yucky feeling again. Bugger off, I want to have a nice day." The feeling would subside, and I'd get on with my day (most of the time). We were health nuts, so we rarely drank alcohol and we exercised like maniacs. That I was in such physical good shape contributed to my ability to manage my panic attacks. A poor diet and alcohol are two of the major contributors to anxiety. Exercise, hydration, and a clean diet help mental health and well-being.

I was excited when I had saved up enough money and I bought my own scuba gear—pink, of course. I had a dive logbook and loved writing my log after each dive. When we'd head out in the boat, my anxiety was always there, but I managed it. Paul would put the boat in the water, and we'd load up our gear and head out to the dive site. Once I got into the water, I felt free—the wet suit, tanks, buoyancy compensator device (which looks like a life vest with all the tubes connecting to the air tanks), and gear were tight and heavy, but once you dropped into the water, you were weightless and free. It was a great feeling. I loved gliding through the kelp and water, watching all the fish swimming around. I used to use up my oxygen a lot quicker than Paul (I called him "part fish"); I breathed faster because of my anxiety. I recall that once, on an amazing dive in the Poor Knights, we were deep, watching the beautiful blue mau-mau fish. I could see my oxygen getting low and got anxious. I pointed to my gauge and showed Paul. He gave me a thumbs up, "all okay." Gesturing, he pulled out his oxygen mouthpiece and handed it to me. "Oh, I see," I thought, "he's suggesting we buddy-breathe. OMG." My oxygen ran out at about thirty meters, and we buddy-breathed all the way to the surface. Far out. It was scary and edgy and cool. What an epic challenge—this is something a dive instructor could lose his license for if found out. Wow, what an achievement—and what a story. I was stepping outside my comfort zone.

I flew on a plane for the first time with Paul when I was twenty-four. He took me to meet his grandmother in Suva, Fiji. The plane trip was pretty uncomfortable—I spent the two-and-a-half-hour flight battling panic and anxiety (claustrophobia; we were stuck in a tin can and I couldn't get out). I vomited, convulsed, and cried. But I made it there and back, and I enjoyed Fiji so much that I vowed to get this panic thing under control so I could enjoy traveling with Paul. In those days, if you had a panic attack, the flight attendant would let you sit next to the pilot. Can you imagine? That was well before September 11, 2001, and on many a flight, I got to be the cute, panicking blonde sitting next to the pilot. You get an epic view up there in the cockpit, and it's a lot less claustrophobic. It was also comforting to chat to the person in charge of the plane. Amazing.

My life with Paul was exciting, and I felt a genuine sense of achievement getting out and about in nature and looking after my health and well-being. We had amazing friends and one of them asked me to be godmother to their little boy—I was blown away. I had real, deep, and meaningful friendships. The universe was delivering. Slowly but surely, I was getting everything on my list. My self-esteem was through the roof. I had a hot boyfriend, and we were going places.

Paul and I had purchased two rental properties, and we had our own home in a suburb close to the city. Our besties and my little godson lived next door to us and we had a lot of fun. My law firm job was a huge part of my life—and even though I worked long hours, I was satisfied. I used to run to the office, get dressed at work, work all day, run to the gym to work out, and then run home and cook a healthy dinner. Life was good. I was happy. Paul was amazing, and I had a fantastic new family. Paul's wonderful set of friends was the icing on the cake. We even had a little Jack Russell dog called Jackie—super original, right?

Paul was not happy with his work. He loved scuba instructing, but we had realized it would not give us the income to carry on building our property portfolio and creating the wealth we wanted. He also got sick of doing it as a job and wanted to keep it as a hobby. He wanted to scuba dive for fun, not work. So, he swapped his wetsuit for a business suit and jumped into the nine-to-five trenches. He was miserable. Our relationship came apart at the seams. I was 100 percent married to my job and fulfilled in every way; Paul hated his job and sat at home after work nagging me to leave the office and come home. We bickered and argued.

Paul needed to do something that lit a fire in his belly. He was a 2nd Dan black belt in karate, in a style that came from Japan, Gōjū-ryū. It was a lifelong dream for him to go to Japan and meet his sensei. It was on his bucket list. By this time, I was pretty stressed out at my job. I had been working until 2:00 a.m. some mornings because the massive apartment buildings project I had been working on was settling. They were monumental achievements for me, but mentally, I was heading for a train crash.

What changed my trajectory was my boss's behavior. At 2:00 a.m. one morning, I was exhausted, and instead of bringing me a cup of tea, he hit on me. I couldn't believe it. First, he knew I was in a serious relationship and second, I was giving this job every ounce of my being. What a wally to want to ruin that. As reluctant as I was to leave the job I adored, after what my boss did, I agreed to go on a trip with Paul to Japan, and to take a break from the law and my beloved boss—with whom I was now angry. My firm threw me a big, fancy farewell party and assured me the job would wait for me until we returned. I was suffering so much FOMO—fear of missing out—walking away from the job and career I had worked so hard to create.

After a long, uncomfortable flight to Japan, fraught with panic attacks and unpleasantness, we landed in Nagoya and headed to our friend Shane's house, where we'd stay until we set ourselves up. I was standing in a freezing, grotty little flat. Snow was falling outside. There was a pet monkey in a cage that stunk the whole place out. I dropped my bags and burst into tears. I wanted to go home … to my beautiful house, my amazing job, my warm country. I had given it all up to help Paul pursue his dream, not mine.

I couldn't even find a decent coffee. I remember searching the next morning for a local coffee shop. We found a vending machine in the street that spat out hot coffee in a can—once I'd figured out how to use it. I felt I'd landed in hell. *What was I was doing here? I* searched my mind and heart, trying to keep the panic under control. *What was the universe trying to tell me? Was it a lesson to pursue my own dreams, not someone else's? Was it a lesson in compromising and supporting my partner? Perhaps,* I thought, *the universe was telling me I didn't need to always be in a relationship.* Everything I'd done since age seventeen had either been wrapped around a partner or had been in pursuit of a different partner. Yes, that was it—I didn't enjoy being on my own and had gone from one relationship to another. I needed to spend time on my own, find out what lit me up. While I was happy for Paul to have pursued his dream to find his Sensei, for the first time in my life, I believed that I'd be better off on my own. In fact, I couldn't wait to be on my own. However, for now, I was trapped in Japan, in the snow, tasked with finding a job and somewhere to live.

Finding My Feet

Like anything in my life, I made the most of an unpleasant situation. Our dire circumstances made us get it together super quick. Manifesting at a hundred miles an hour kicked in. New flat: done. New job: done. Beautiful apartment decked out: done. Righto, I'm living in Japan. No friends, family, or support. Anxiety? On high alert. Panic attacks? Plenty. The winter was extreme; I'd never experienced cold like it. If that wasn't bad enough, wait for summer—it was so hot the following summer in Japan, my hair started to fall out.

Don't get me wrong—there were a lot of wonderful positives about Japan. I loved the scenery—the cherry blossom festivals and season were a highlight. My favorite pastime was visiting the amazing Buddhist temples and learning about the Buddha. I found a wonderful yoga studio run by a lovely chap called Tatsu and started going often. I think Tatsu enjoyed the *Gaijings* (Japanese word for foreigners) that came to see him. His English benefited from our visits as much as our Japanese benefited from listening to him speak to us in Japanese.

The break from law was good. I was teaching English at the Berlitz English Academy; we were earning huge money. It was another thing that helped keep me sane, watching these vast sums of money landing in my bank account for doing not a lot; speaking English to Japanese business people. So, the riches were there, but the unhappiness was there as well. Paul was in heaven. I was in hell.

Paul became possessive and jealous. My fellow teachers and I often worked until 10:00 p.m., when the last business executives finished their lessons. Often, all the teachers would head to the local *Izakaya* pub and have a few drinks. The teachers were from all around the world and were often highly educated people from different professions. But teaching English in Japan paid better than being a neurologist or a surgeon—crazy but true. One teacher, Izac, was French … very French. He talked openly about sex. One night, he asked me an inappropriate personal question. OMG. It was pretty "in-your-face"—I was embarrassed at his openness. Paul went into a jealous rage. He went mental. He blamed me for flirting with Izac and leading him on. For goodness' sake, as if I could control what came out of the Frenchman's mouth. We went home, and the torment went on long into the night. At 2:00 a.m., I considered throwing myself off the ninth floor of the building just to stop the mental torture. The next day, I had to get up early and start a three-hour trek to a girls' university I was teaching at once a week. I remember being exhausted, emotionally and physically, and having to stand up in front of thirty Japanese girls and pretend to be happy and engaging. I wanted to die. It was the longest day in history for me. I was at the end of my tether.

After nine months of teaching English in Japan, we had saved a huge nest egg in our bank accounts. Our plan was to go on the OE (overseas excursion) of all OEs. We were not planning to backpack. We were going all out, staying in beautiful places in gorgeous cities and going on expensive, planned trips—not the Kon-Tiki expedition all our friends back home had done. Our relationship was in tatters, and the trip was what we both needed.

At the end of the trip, the plan was that I would spend a few weeks on my own with my sisters (who were by then living in the UK), and then head back to Japan to meet up with Paul. This was my chance … I planned my escape. Once I was safely with my sisters in the UK, I had no intention of ever going back to Japan. I felt like a double-agent spy planning a mission.

Having decided to leave Paul (although he didn't know it), I had a great time on our Cosmos tour, which took us, among other places, through Frankfurt, down the Rhine River on a barge, and to Rome, Florence, Orvieto, and Venice. We had our moments for sure, but mostly, we had a great time. There were so many times I had to pinch myself—the shy little girl from Ramarama was walking through the streets of Venice, shopping, eating, and taking in the sights—not a panic attack in sight. I'll never forget standing in Venice square. I closed my eyes and said to the universe, "One day, I'll come back here with my real soulmate."

Rags to Riches Tip – Repeat the Experience

Have you had a situation like this, when you wanted to repeat the experience another time with another person? Did you ever go back?

What is the one place you would like to return to with a special person? Write down the dream and put a timeline on it. Or perhaps add it to your dream board.

I haven't made it back to Venice yet, but I will … with my Mark.

Landing in Rome at the end of our trip, I remember going up the escalator, looking down at Paul below. He was waving. I waved back. Tears rolled down my cheeks as the escalator took me farther and farther away from him. It was goodbye. I knew it; he didn't. I headed to my sister Jojo's home in the UK. Phew. I was safe. Paul and I exchanged emails, and it was via email I told him I had no intention of coming back to Japan to pick up where we had left off. He was kind—he packed up my things and send them home to New Zealand, to my parents' house. As far as I'm aware, he's still in Japan today.

Panic and anxiety are strange. Someone once said to me, "You'll never have a panic attack in a situation in which the attack will cause you to die." For example, you won't have one while you're driving. So, panic attacks hit when you are safe … like it's safe to panic. That's what happened when I got to the safety and comfort of Jojo's home in the UK. I unraveled. The nine months of stress and anxiety of holding it all together in Japan came out. I couldn't eat, sleep, or relax. The weight plummeted off me—I was a tiny sixty-five-kilograms (143 pounds) in a five-foot ten body—a far cry from the eighty-five-kilogram (187 pounds), overweight, miserable human being that had left Japan. It was like I was being shredded to the bone. Sixty-five kilograms may not sound tiny, but on my frame, it is. I'm tall. When I put on weight, it all goes on around my middle and my arms and legs stay long and skinny—so it's dangerous for me to gain weight.

I could put the weight I had gained with Paul down to a few

reasons: emotional protection, cortisol, and antidepressants. Emotions live in the belly, and belly fat wraps around your organs as a protection layer to guard you from being kicked in the guts, so to speak. Another reason for central obesity is the release of the stress hormone cortisol (of which I had plenty). I'd been taking antidepressants, which slowed down my metabolism. So, in the UK, in a safe environment with low stress, I got into a routine which allowed me to stop taking anti-depressants, replacing them instead with adrenal support vitamins and St. John's Wort. My meditations focused on letting go of emotional baggage, helping me release the tummy fat protection. Daily yoga was another tool in my conquering stress toolbox, which assisted my body, mind, and soul to release old, stuck negative energy, fat, and stress. I addressed all three reasons (medication, emotional, and physical stress) I blamed for my weight gain.

Real Me Action – Recognizing Rescuers

Journal Entry # 1 – September 2001

"Said goodbye to my old life and arrived in London." A spiritual teacher once said to me that our rescuers can sometimes come in the form of a shark. But at the time we don't realize they are, in fact, a rescuer and not a shark after all.

Can you relate to weight gain triggers like medication, emotional upset, or physical stress? Get quiet and comfortable with your journal. Write down all the situations in which you have been triggered to eat unhealthy food or fall back into old eating habits.

- *Emotional protection.*
- *Antidepressant medication.*
- *Cortisol stress hormones.*

72

Baby Heather with her three older siblings.

The home Heather grew up in from 1971 to 2001.

Heather with little Harrison - my reason to push through the darkest of days.

*School photo of Heather wearing a handmade
tartan pinafore dress.*

To dear Heather

May Beloved Baba help you to
feel His presence more and more
during your stay at Meherazad

With best wishes,
Bal Natu

A personal letter from Bal Natu from Meherazad India.
He would have been a very elderly man when he wrote this to
me in October 2007.

*The Avatar Meher Baba Indian spiritual master standing on top of
Seclusion Hill in India prior to his death in 1969.*

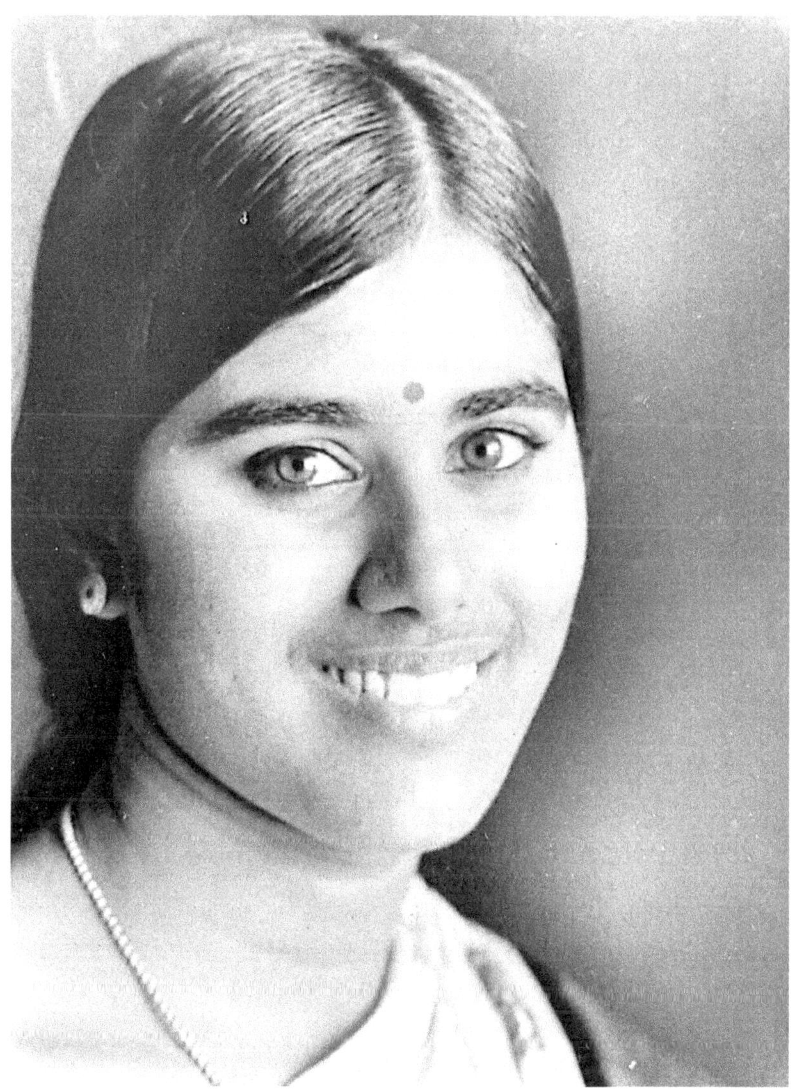

Mother Meera the Divine Mother.

Heather's students at the Girls University in Japan 2006.

The Humber 80 Heather traveled in order to get from Puna, India, to Meher Baba's Ashram.

82

Chapter Five:

Eating, Praying, and Loving

Going on My Spiritual Journey

The flip side to the situation in the UK is that I looked and felt amazing in my new sixty-five-kilogram body ... LOL. Jojo was wonderful. I couldn't have been in a better place to unravel so spectacularly. By now, Jojo had stepped into her calling as a lightworker, giving long-distance readings for clients all over the world. She was clairvoyant and a real spiritual therapist. Just what I needed. People would email or call her for a reading and when the time was right and her clairvoyance kicked in, she would do an incredible reading and send the client a CD. Sometimes clients would have to wait up to a year for a reading from Jojo. I was in awe. She was living her Truth and helping others at the same time.

A man named Marcus, a friend of Jojo and her husband, was a tower of support and strength for me. I had plenty of cash from my savings in Japan. I had an instant and overwhelming attraction to Marcus and thought, "Oh no, here I go again. Out of one relationship, into another." Even Jojo warned me: "Don't you hurt Marcus, he's a great guy and has been through a lot." It turned out that Marcus's ex-wife was making accusations about his treatment of their children, which were not true—Marcus would never hurt a fly. I was appalled that a woman would use her children like pawns in a game. It was horrific. The poor wee kids missed their dad terribly. Marcus told me his little girl, Georgia, used to get insecure at night and feel homesick. I couldn't believe it. She was exactly like me. The first time I stayed at Marcus's house, I shook like someone in sub-zero temperatures all night and felt sick. I was right back to being a homesick five-year-old. It was like being around Georgia was triggering me big time.

Marcus and I decided that since we both had past baggage we needed to offload, we would go on a spiritual trip to India and leave it behind. Our purpose was to find ourselves and spend some amazing time together in the motherland of India. I had lost so much weight, I was dreading a plane trip and feeling sick and anxious. Reading my journals from that time, it was interesting that I described the flight as "lovely," so I must have controlled my panic.

We flew to Bombay (Mumbai) and stayed overnight in a hotel called the Leela. I'd experienced nothing like it. It was a six-star hotel—and opulent! Men with gold turbans opened the door and all the chandeliers were over the top. Spectacular shops in the basement sold hand-stitched, amazing jewel-encrusted tapestries. Yet just outside the door, there were people in the gutter and the mud, living on the side of the road, and begging to survive. I felt sad, but was also blown away and happy. *India is a country of contradictions and contrasts.* The next day, we took an internal flight from Bombay to Pune and were picked up in an old white Humber 80 with ancient suspension. We bounced along the dusty road for an hour to Meherabad—the place where, in 1923, the Avatar Meher Baba ("compassionate father") established an ashram. As we got closer to Meherabad, we could feel the energy building. Some of Baba's original followers were still alive and living in the Meherabad village. Jojo had taught me that at any given time, there are fifty-six God-realized people (or avatars) on the planet, but only seven of them make themselves known to everyday people. The rest are scattered around the world, living in the hills in Tibet and elsewhere. Meher Baba was one of the seven and although he had passed away in 1969, they said that his spirit and his energy would remain on earth for 100 years. So, visiting Meherabad had the same spiritual profundity as visiting another living avatar whose energy was, among many things, therapeutic to the soul. Visiting and helping do the daily work in his tomb (otherwise known as "the Samadhi," which means "very religious place of enlightenment") was as good as being in his presence.

A daily ritual began. We rose at 6:30 a.m. and headed to the Samadhi for Arti (Prayers). Everything was so organized and peaceful. They had gentle rules and regulations so that the tomb was never over-crowded, and you could stay and meditate for as long as you liked. I remember being told once that the teachings of yoga were so that you could train your body to sit in meditation for hours or even days at a time. So, I practiced this every day, extending the time I spent in lotus pose in the tomb, reciting the Great Invocation over and over in my head. "The Great Invocation" is an ancient prayer, directed by the Hierarchy for the benefit of the humanity, to request the Divine energies for renewing and reviving our Planet. It was conceived to bring down Divine Light, Divine Love, and Divine Power on Earth.

The Great Invocation

From the point of Light within the Mind of God

Let light stream forth into the minds of men.

Let Light descend on Earth.

From the point of Love within the Heart of God

Let love stream forth into the hearts of men.

May Christ return to Earth.

From the center where the Will of God is known

Let purpose guide the little wills of men –

The purpose which the Masters know and serve.

From the center which we call the race of men

Let the Plan of Love and Light work out

And may it seal the door where evil dwells.

Let light and love and Power restore the Plan on Earth.[12]

Staying in the ashram was strange at first. There was a "women's" and a "men's" side. Marcus was on one side of the ashram; I was on the other. We slept on little metal bunks with other people who were on their own journeys. My roommate was a lovely girl named Melinda. It was nice to have some good company. The little metal bunks had mosquito nets around them and at night, I meditated on my bunk.

Marcus was an angel—I'd never experienced being looked after the way he looked after me. He'd bring me water and cups of Indian sweet tea. After meals, he would take my plate back to the kitchen and was always checking that I was okay. I was not used

---

[12]"The Great Invocation," Share International, July 16, 2022, https://www.share-international.org/background/xmission/tm_invocation.htm.

to this and felt myself getting uptight about being treated nicely. Isn't that crazy? I got the love and attention I'd always wanted and was resisting it—the "unworthy me" was trying to push him away. Marcus and I spent a lot of time talking about our lives and what we had gone through until that point. When I look back on my journal writings from this time with him in the ashram, I had made an entry:

> One day at the ashram, I was talking to Marcus about happiness and it occurred to me I'd never been happy in my life. Not as a child, not as a teenager, not as a young woman in her twenties. Then we both cried. It was amazing to let that unhappiness out. I could write an entire book on happiness, but happiness starts from within. So, because until now I'd never been able to love myself, I just did not know how to experience true happiness.

> There was quite a routine for each day at the ashram: breakfast, meditation, yoga, heading up to the tomb and cleaning it, then more yoga, singing, teachings, eating, and meditating. Cleaning the tomb was a daily, complex process; I suppose it was their way of honoring Baba and showing their love and respect for him even in death: the gentle wiping down of every tile around his shrine, gentle dusting, placing flowers, then singing and worshiping. The days drifted by. I wrote several full journals of my thoughts and memories while at Meherabad.

My meditation practice and experience were heightened in the ashram. I've never felt closer to God or the universe, or to knowing what happiness and contentment mean. My faith that everything was as it should be had never been stronger. I felt I was at a point of neutrality, almost like I had resolved every past struggle I'd ever had in life. My foundation was solid; I knew I could move into the future, knowing I could have or be anything I wanted to be or create.

Despite knowing I could achieve anything material I wanted, it cost a pound a day to live in the ashram. I didn't see the point in going back to the UK, or even back to New Zealand as there wasn't a single thing I could name that I wanted. Everything I could ever want was right there with me, inside me. For the first time in my life, I was all I needed. I was enough. The people in Meherabad were content with having very little and I could be, too. I could let go of that awful feeling I'd had growing up with needing material things and a stunning home to feel worthy. The Meherabad residents felt blessed. They had everything they ever needed, and couldn't want for anything. Some of them had been visitors like I was and had never left. It was tempting.

Rags to Riches Tip – Practice Daily Gratitude

A huge lesson in gratitude here—start small. A great practice is to wake up every day and start your daily ritual. Grab your journal and start by writing three headings. I've included some examples to get you started.

"Today, I am grateful for:

- my gorgeous husband and children.
- the roof over my head and the food I have to eat.
- our little puppy who brings us such joy."

"For today to be wonderful, the following things will happen:

- I will write a thousand words of my book.
- I will have that awkward conversation with Jenny at work and it will have a great outcome.
- I will make that call to my brother I've been meaning to make for ages."

Affirmations to Myself:

- "I am strong and beautiful and deserve all the happiness in the world."
- "I am a kind person and I have a lot to share with others."
- "I am worthy of love and all the good things that come my way."

- *"I accept myself for who I am and love myself unconditionally."*

You get the picture. Start small. Start ticking off your achievements, and in time, your happiness will grow because you are acknowledging the things the universe is providing to you.

One thing I never forget is that if you are ungrateful or not thankful for what people give you, they will stop giving things to you. The universe is the same. If you take it for granted or don't express your gratitude and appreciation, you won't get any more. We all know people who just appear to be takers. They never give back. There are many ways to describe these people, including as "energy vampires." They don't contribute or even see the purpose in saying "Thank you." Their worlds remain small so their hearts remain small. They are unfulfilled and, ultimately, they are unhappy. I feel so much sadness and pity for such people. Take a huge breath and expand your heart with gratitude and appreciation, and let it come back to you tenfold. Woo hoo! It's exhilarating.

When you do this journaling exercise, on some days you will write for ages, and on other days, you may answer the three questions under your headings, and then get on with life. The key is consistency, creating that daily ritual. It's fun and reviewing your old journals can provide huge healing and recognition. You can see how far you've come—and sometimes, you'll discover little golden reminders and gifts from the past.

Taking the New Me Home

There were other newcomers in Meherabad who had lived in the ashram for years. Like me, they had come to India on their own journey to heal, learn, or to "eat, pray, love," as I had, but they never left. In lots of ways, as I said earlier, I didn't see the point in going back to western civilization—I'd only be walking back into a world that focused on success, money, and climbing corporate and social ladders. My panic attacks had left me almost entirely in India; I was at peace with everything. Even if I felt a panic attack coming on once in a while, it just manifested as tummy butterflies. I was having the ultimate *eat pray love* experience. But a big part of me was frightened to stay in this world, and the comfort and familiarity of home beckoned. I had to face the music. I felt like I might want to go home with the newfound gratitude and appreciation I had learned and start living my best life back in New Zealand.

All too soon, our planned time at Meherabad ended. The reality of staying on my own there was too scary and a much bigger step than I was willing to take. So, Marcus and I left our sanctuary and headed back to the UK.

Before I left India, I went down the road to a tiny library in the middle of nowhere. It had a computer where you could log in and check emails. I'd had an email from Paul. I was shocked. He was arriving in India that very day to do his own *India "eat, pray, love."* I couldn't believe it! In our earlier email exchanges when I was back in the UK, I must have mentioned I was planning a trip to India. I was overjoyed that he was going to work on himself and start his own spiritual journey. Paul said that the shock of my leaving him had triggered him to want to be a better person and to heal the hurt of his own past. But Paul and I were like a stick that had been broken and could never be mended. For me, that door had closed, but hearing that he was turning the hurt into healing brought me such joy. Paul was going to another of the seven God-realized avatars, Sai Baba's ashram in Puttaparthi. It's interesting, because Sai Baba has different energy from any of the other avatars, and he wasn't an avatar I was drawn to at that time. It was Paul's journey and I let him—and India—go with love. I walked back to the ashram alone, thinking about Paul. Part of me was sad that it took breaking up for us both to do such incredible work on ourselves, but part of me felt overjoyed that my beloved Paul had found his way back to himself. And now, it was time for me to take the me I'd become at Meherabad back home to England (or New Zealand). Marcus and I walked away from the ashram to the Humber 80 that was waiting to take us to the airport, our souls full and our hearts full of hope for all the wonderful things our new life would bring.

Flying on planes was getting better for me. Still terrified of having a panic attack, I would panic about panicking. It wasn't the idea of flying that set me off, it was the fear of having a panic attack. They are horrific—when most people first experience one, they think they are dying or suffering from some terrible illness. Hormones and adrenals going crazy, sickness, diarrhea, and the racing heart that follows is nothing short of horrendous. It's hard to believe that a response of our sympathetic nervous system, ingrained in our DNA for millennia (the so-called "fight-or-flight" reaction), has such a physiological impact on our bodies. I'd gotten a lot better at acknowledging the feeling of panic, letting it rise and fall, and trying hard not to engage with it or give it the energy or strength to take hold of me. Having spent the last period of my life in India, where no stress or noise from the outside world was present, having a panic attack seemed pointless—almost annoying. I had a conversation with myself: *Haven't you just spent the last few weeks letting go of things that don't serve you? How does overthinking this serve you? I have too many recent positive, happy memories to let unhelpful, irrelevant, catastrophic thinking destroy my happiness.* I closed my eyes and imagined Meherabad and its beautiful people. I went into a state of meditation, almost asleep, gently running memories, experiences, and moments of love and kindness over the past few weeks through my mind. The panic was gone, and with a smile on my face, I leaned over snuggled into Marcus's big arm and drifted off to sleep, excited about the next chapter of life.

Rags to Riches Tip – Flip a Negative to a Positive

Interrupt the negative and engage the positive. What is your go-to in a stressful situation? Let's interrupt negative thought patterns at every opportunity, and switch it for a positive.

Every time you find your mind drifting to a negative or starting a sentence with:

"I hate" ... Or "Oh no, not again," ... switch any negative engagement, to a positive and change it to "I love" ... "Oh yay, I'm going to ...."

96

Chapter Six

Flip-Flopping – NZ or UK?

Going Home

Back at Jojo's in the UK, I didn't want our *India "eat, pray, love"* experience to end. The thought of going home to New Zealand was still there, but I wanted to make the most of the spiritual journey I had started. So, what next? I had a wonderful opportunity to be in the presence of another of the seven God realized people on Earth, an Indian Spiritual leader named Mata Amritanandamayi Devi, though everyone calls her Amma. She is known as "the hugging saint." Having had such a beautiful experience in India, I was well and truly open to having another one.

Amma gave darshan as often as she could, which meant that even being in her presence was as close as you could get to God on earth (or your version of what God is for you). To be honest, I was skeptical. Visiting a dead guru's grave was one thing but being in the presence of a living avatar raised both excitement and fear in my belly. I went to darshan with Marcus, and we took our place in the huge auditorium and waited. In the distance, we could hear Indian spiritual music and beautiful chanting and drums. As Amma and her followers got closer and closer to the auditorium, and the music got louder and louder, the butterflies in my tummy stirred. My level of excitement rose. *What was going to happen?*

The momentum and the energy in the auditorium grew to blow-your-mind awesomeness. By the time I saw Amma, the joy in my heart just blew up and overflowed. I burst into tears of joy in the presence of this spectacular, selfless human being. To this day, I've never felt like this—it was like having a spiritual orgasm— seriously. You probably think I'm mad. But it gave me a taste of what it was like to believe in God and that he/she/they/it exists (in whatever form you believe in). I touched it that day—and it touched me back.

Amma took her place at the front of the auditorium, seated on the hard, cold floor. She was a tiny Indian woman wrapped in robes. Her smile lit up the entire room. Her followers chanted as Amma began her darshan of hugging people. A huge line had formed in front of her, which Marcus and I joined. This selfless creature gave maternal darshan hugs until she was no longer able to because of her back pain. When it was our turn, she gathered Marcus and me to her chest, one of us in each arm and embraced us together like we were the first person she had ever hugged. I can't even describe how this felt but again I dissolved into tears. In that moment, I felt like she had healed so many old scars and wounds in my little twenty-nine-year-young being. Her love was unconditional and left such a feeling of true happiness. They say when she hugs you as a couple, she also heals you as a couple and speeds up your karma.

Thus ended my Indian love affair. Amma's embrace had reminded me of Mom and Dad. I'd been away from home about a year and I wanted to check up on them—Dad was in his seventies and Mom was in her sixties. By some miracle (or should I say "by my manifestation superpower in action"), I had conjured up a trade whereby Mom and Dad swapped their unsaleable, run-down farm for a little house in town. It was a shame that a ten-acre block of land was only worth as much as a small house in an average little town, but it was what it was and it was my parents' journey, not mine. The farm was so run down and there was so much work to do—that work would never get done while my parents owned it. Trading for a quarter-acre section in the suburbs was the right thing to do. I was still holding on to the residue of wanting to fix their house and their lives so I could be proud to bring people over, but I had concluded that it wasn't what they wanted and India had taught me It just didn't matter. So, I booked a return trip from London to New Zealand to help with the mammoth task of moving them from the farm into town.

Going home was great. I loved seeing Mom and Dad. I'd let go of so much old hurt and unworthiness of my own that I could just enjoy my time with them. I could even relax in their mess having no attachment to it or having a burning desire to fix it. I was having such a good time, I thought about staying in New Zealand. I loved catching up with all my old mates at the law firm and I fell back into the clubbing, boozing, partying lifestyle that was in alignment with my old life (and out of alignment with what I was trying to create as my new life).

One night, I partied hard with my pals. I woke up the next day with a hangover and thought, *What am I doing?* I panicked. *OMG, I'm falling back into that old life.* I hadn't yet canceled my return flight back to the UK—it was that day at 5:00 p.m. Looking back now, it was hilarious. I threw my belongings into a suitcase. My poor elderly parents were flapping around scooping up after me. Remember the kid who was the "fart in the bottle," tearing from one thing to another? "Rip, shit, and bust" my mom used to say. This was all-too-familiar behavior from me, and Mom and Dad were used to it. "It's Heather's way or the highway." We bundled into the car and took off to the airport. The Air New Zealand customer service agent at check-in asked me to pack my bag—half my clothes were jammed and hanging out the side of my case. Hugging my baffled (but strangely proud) elderly Mom and Dad, off I went, back on a twenty-four-hour flight path to the UK. My phone rang when I was transiting LAX. It was my friend in NZ asking me, "What are you up to tonight?" He was shocked when I replied, "Ah, I'm in LA, en route to the UK."

I turned thirty on that plane, somewhere between New Zealand and London. I was alone and confused about where I wanted to be and how I fit into this world. At the time, Nelly Furtado was number one on the charts with her song, *I'm Like a Bird*.[13] Like her, I didn't know where my soul or my home were. Couldn't have been more fitting. I listened to the song on my headphones and bawled my eyes out.

Back in the UK, I tried to settle down. I applied for jobs but got nothing. Compared to NZ, things in the UK seemed to move at a snail's pace. It was September 2001. I was sitting in Jojo's lounge in London watching in disbelief (like most of the world at the time) as the September 11 terrorist attacks unfolded live on television. I wanted to go home. It didn't feel right for me to be this far from Mom and Dad, from the life that I had been reminded of back in NZ. If I hadn't gone back to NZ, I wouldn't have been thinking about it. As the craziness of the 911 events unfolded, I missed familiarity. The homesickness I'd felt as a child had come back, and deep down, I realized I was a bit of a "homebody" and liked to be near my parents. So, I booked a flight back to New Zealand—this

---

[13] Nelly Furtado, "I'm Like a Bird," track 1 on *Whoa, Nelly!* DreamWorks, 2000, compact disc, https://www.youtube.com/watch?v=roPQ_M3yJTA.

time, a one-way ticket. In a space of four weeks, I'd gone from London to Auckland, Auckland to London, and London to Auckland. That was a lot of toxic airplane energy swimming around in my fragile, confused body. I was told once by a spiritual teacher that it takes nine months to get the bad energy of a two-hour plane flight out of your system—so I had a deluge of magnetic waves in my body built up from my UK to NZ flip-flopping. On the upside, I was becoming a seasoned traveler, and panic attacks on planes were becoming less of a thing.

I went back to stay with Mom and Dad, and they were thrilled. I was home again. I went back to my old legal job, back to climbing the corporate ladder, back to the financial treadmill. My *eat pray love* memories faded.

Real Me Action – Wasting Time or Learning Lessons

Was it time wasted, or lessons learned? Time is only wasted if you don't learn from an experience.

Think of a situation in which you made tremendous progress, only to turn around and undo it all. Perhaps, for example, you lost weight after weeks of eating well and exercising, only to eat terribly again, stopping your exercise routine—and undoing all your hard work.

Now write your end goal on your goals list. What do you want to achieve? This time, do it for life, not for a moment in time. Make a lifelong commitment to achieve and keep this goal.

Next, grab your journal and write five things you can do today towards achieving that goal. Read it daily and commit to making that change for good.

Hindsight Is a Wonderful Thing

To this day, it amazes me how I had refused to look at the signals the universe was giving me. I know that my entire life is perfect, and that everything has happened in divine, perfect timing. Even though I'm writing this now, knowing that, looking back at what I put myself through to be the person I am today still blows me away. But I wouldn't be the person I am today unless it had all happened … so I suppose it's moot.

Funny, looking back … within a few weeks of arriving home in NZ, I received an email from a London law firm offering me a job I'd applied for and really wanted. But it was too late. I was starting over in Auckland. The NZ legal firm re-employed me as a business development manager, not as a legal executive. This was a promotion, and it felt great to be in a senior management position, earning substantial money again. I'd been away for a year and a few new clients had joined the firm. It was my job to foster those relationships and attract more business in the form of new clients.

A new client, Kevin, had joined the firm. He wasn't handsome, but he had caught my eye. He had a presence about him and I noticed he'd stare at me when he was in the office. I was polite and offered my help whenever I saw him. Then dozens of red roses arrived in my office, followed by texts and phone calls asking me to go out with him. I was flattered, but he was a lot older than me, so I turned his requests down, saying that I wasn't interested in dating. He was persistent, and at a lonely moment, I said "Yes." After that, things moved so fast, my head spun off. Dinners, champagne, gifts, outings, functions, more gifts—within three months we had rented a beautiful penthouse apartment together, close to where I worked. Wow! I had landed on my feet—or so I thought.

Little did I know that the next seven years would nearly kill me.

The cycle of abuse is subtle. Anyone who has ever had a gaslighting or narcissistic relationship and survived it will attest to how it creeps up on you. Friends and family can be judgmental, saying, "How could you stay in that abusive relationship? Why didn't you just leave?" But it happens slowly. It gets ever so slightly worse and worse. Not only does it creep up on you, but you start to believe you deserve this, that it's not that bad.

The signs were all there. I just didn't see them. The universe was trying to tell me something, but I wasn't listening. The late nights of dinners and drinking took their toll. Even though they'd gotten better, I'd still have panic attacks on a plane, train, boat, or some sort of public transport, or when I was enclosed in claustrophobic spaces. My fight-or-flight antenna would go up and off I'd go into panic mode.

I remember the day everything started to unravel. Work had always been my safe place, my haven, my mental sanctuary. I could keep my mind busy, go into a cocoon, and side-track my thoughts. I was safe there. But ... uh oh ... on this day, it all hit me like a freight train. I was sitting at my desk with a hangover when the panic rose. It was like a wave of warm water and nausea coming from the pit of my stomach, up through my chest. My chest tightened, my throat closed, and my mind caved into catastrophic thoughts. I was sobbing, out of control, desperate for air. The office rang for an ambulance. I thought I was dying. My heart was racing. I was squirming, writhing, and grabbing at my throat. The panic was overwhelming. The last thing I remember, I was in the ambulance, being tranquilized and knocked out.

The following six weeks were hell, as I tried and failed to get this horrific feeling under control. The doctors gave me several medications, none of which suited me. They took days to work, and then I'd discover they just made things worse. I was medicated—at least to where I could function. I went back to work medicated, with the panic masked and my anxiety bottled up, the lid screwed on tight. From the outside looking in, everything appeared normal.

Looking back now, I know the universe was trying to warn me,

"Heather, you've taken a wrong turn. This path will not serve you or your soul journey—get out." I was at a crossroads. *Do I turn left and follow the spiritual journey I started in India, where I had woken up my soul to a spiritual path of being neutral towards money? Or do I turn right and take what appears to be a path of glamour, shiny new things, and a life I had dreamed of for years, living in a home I was proud of?* I even called Jojo, my spiritual sister, for advice: "Which path should I take?" But like any spiritual guru, she wouldn't give me an answer because it was my decision to make. She said that "There's no right or wrong path, there is a life lesson at the end of each path, so it's not possible to make a wrong choice."

So, on I went. I stayed on anti-anxiety medication for years. Kevin was not wealthy when I met him, but he had huge aspirations and an uncanny ability to see things others didn't. I knew together we could manifest anything material we wanted. He was mildly spiritual and wasn't alarmed by the meditation and positive affirmations I was doing. But he didn't encourage them either, and soon doing my lovely daily rituals became a thing of the past. Instead, I opted for dinners out and a large glass of Pinot Noir.

Kevin had been a partner in a property development company that was building a commercial building with a row of penthouses on top. He had planned to keep one penthouse for himself from the profits. It was fun being involved in the project. Kevin made me feel important, asking me to help choose tiles and finishes. He had great style and taste and the whole penthouse was coming together. We had Phillipe Stark Crystal jar pendants in the entranceway, tiny white mosaic tiles, and slate tiles on the floor. The Italian kitchen was a dream, and it was a fit for a princess. So, when it was finished, we moved from our rented apartment into the new penthouse. It was like a mansion to me—everything brand new, white, and stunning, with all the latest and greatest fixtures and fittings. I never cooked in the kitchen, though. More often than not, we had the Japanese restaurant downstairs make our meals.

Kevin had three daughters from a previous marriage that had ended a few years earlier and he was keen for me to have my own child. Until then, I hadn't thought of having a child. It wasn't something high on my radar—because my childhood had put me off the idea of bringing a child into the world, but also because I had never felt secure enough financially. Kevin insisted it was something I needed to do, given that he already had his girls. As far as he was concerned, I needed my own child. Within a year of meeting him, I was pregnant with our son.

At that stage, I left the job I loved. Kevin encouraged me to start a business, which was wonderful. The building we lived in (in Parnell, Auckland) had a commercial level below our apartment, and there was still some space left to lease out. I was three months pregnant when I opened the doors to my new firm—Via Property. I was so proud; I loved our little pink logo. We were consultants to property developers, filling in gaps in their infrastructure that they couldn't afford to (or didn't want to) carry the costs of while building their huge buildings. We were like administrative support to developers. Often, a developer would have only a small team (of men, mainly) who worked on the funding of the build project and on the construction side of things. They fell short of having people to liaise with the salespeople in charge of selling down their product. They needed someone to look after all their buyers and to keep these customers up-to-date, from the day they purchased off the plans until the day the apartment was built. The role even involved taking buyers through the completed apartments, making sure they were happy with the end product, and ensuring they would pay the settlement funds when it was time to move in. We did all of this for our clients so they could focus on what they did best, the financing and construction of the buildings.

We charged a thousand dollars a unit. So, for example, if a building had 300 units, my fee was $300,000. The fee was divided by the period of construction, say twelve months, and was paid to us by the funders of the project. It was a colossal hit and a tremendous success. I made it a no-brainer, so our fees were built into project funding. By the time the funding kicked into place and we were getting paid, our hard work was done, and I sat back and watched the monthly fees roll in. I was so proud of what I had put together. It was a brilliant business model with low overhead.

I'd employed a young woman to work alongside me and she ended up becoming my sanity. She would witness what was going on between me and Kevin—and didn't like it. Often, I asked her,

"Did that really happen?" My brain was mush. I was confused, stressed, and I couldn't remember a lot of what had happened.

I was now heavily pregnant and Kevin, my baby daddy, was going great guns with his property projects. My company ended up consulting mainly to his company, and my little pride-and-joy business merged with his and we were building a soon-to-be-huge property portfolio. With the baby nearly due, it suited me to be under the umbrella of our property company. It carried the costs of my business and I could continue to work without the financial overhead to be worried about.

I have skimmed over the details of the earlier days in my relationship with Kevin—just like I'd done in my own mind at the time—blurring and shaking off unrest and things that didn't sit right, reconciling them, telling myself, "It's not so bad, I must have gotten it wrong. Keep calm and carry on. All will be well." But in the early days of meeting Kevin, some weird things happened. I swept them under the carpet, shrugged them off. For example, he used to go to the supermarket for hours. I used to joke about him having an affair with the supermarket. A few people came up to me out of nowhere and told me, "Kevin is engaged to another woman." It seemed far-fetched; I ignored them. *They've got it wrong, that can't be right.* People are just making trouble. I got some strange phone calls from a woman with an American accent. She called herself Chrissy and claimed she was engaged to Kevin. Lots of blocked number, hang-up calls happened. I was blind to the truth (as it would later unfold).

I did a little research. Chrissy existed. Kevin had, in fact, been dating a woman called Chrissy. He had lied to me. They weren't engaged, he said—she was a nutter and a stalker and had made up a lot of stories. One afternoon, Kevin and I were having lunch in a restaurant with friends and a beautiful blonde woman stormed up to our table and yelled at Kevin that she had been waiting for him to arrive and he hadn't turned up. Then she stormed away. We all laughed it off, and Kevin told me again that she was crazy. Many years later, however, I learned the truth: He was in fact engaged to her! She was unpopular with his children, they didn't like her. She was a loud lady with a strong American accent (which stood out in little old New Zealand). She dressed boldly—and, again, that wasn't well accepted in New Zealand. Kevin said he had become bored with her overpowering personality and wanted to move on. What he hadn't done, however, was break up with her—he had moved in with me and continued to lie to both of us and live a double life. I don't know how long our relationships with him crossed over, but looking back, there were at least three to six months of weird behavior—no doubt the result of Kevin juggling his two relationships.

While I was pregnant, there were lots of late nights with me at home alone with my bump. One night, after having dinner at a bar near our apartment, I went home early. I was quite pregnant and got tired easily. I was still taking antidepressants (I was told they wouldn't affect my unborn baby). Kevin said, "See you in an hour." I woke up at midnight with a start—he still wasn't home. So, I went back to the bar and found him ... slow dancing cheek-to-cheek with a friend of mine. The stressful situation that unfolded that night was something no one should have to go through, let alone a pregnant working momma. I walked up to Kevin, punched him in the face, and stormed off home. Of course, he denied that anything had happened between them. But the trouble was, this friend had been having an affair with a high-profile married man for many years. Having an affair with my partner would not have bothered her in the slightest. I knew this because I was her flat mate when I came back to NZ, and her lover would sneak in and out of our flat. Somehow, as usual, Kevin talked his way out of the situation, made me feel stupid for reacting the way I did, and life carried on.

My beautiful son was two weeks overdue. I don't blame him for not wanting to come out into the real world. When he was born, I held him in my arms and felt a love like no other for this little being. My gratitude was immense. I was so grateful that I had been talked into having a baby. My baby boy. We named him James. All I wanted to do was protect this little soul and give him a life that I didn't have. You've heard that before, right?

A lot of what happened with Kevin I've buried deep inside and remembering it isn't helpful. But it was the typical cycle: an abusive event would happen, followed by love, gifts, kindness, regret ... then ramping up again to his usual ways, until he would pop again and be abusive, followed by love, gifts, kindness, and so on—rinse-and-repeat. Each time the mental abuse happened, the physical abuse got worse and worse. I had become an expert in playing music in James' nursery so he wouldn't hear the shouting. Kevin even punched a big hole in the nursery wall above James' cot, knowing it would destroy me.

Kevin's control issues even extended to him risking James' life. One of the worst days of my life was one morning when I first discovered James was asthmatic. He was only ten months old. He was turning blue and foaming at the mouth. I was screaming at Kevin to call an ambulance, but he insisted instead on driving James to the hospital, saying I was overreacting. I even rang our family doctor while in the car who said, "Why are you driving? You need an ambulance with the equipment he needs on board." We were stuck in peak-hour traffic that morning and I was desperate to get him on a ventilator, find out what the heck was wrong, and save our boy's life. Just one more example of Kevin's control that affected my mental health (and that nearly ended my son's life). Finally, we got to hospital, James was rushed into emergency, and they put an oxygen mask on him to get air into his lungs. He was treated for over twelve hours to get the asthma under control. It was awful.

Despite the ongoing mental abuse, Kevin and I got married when James was one year old. It was a beautiful wedding. We held it in a boutique lodge, and I arrived in a horse-drawn carriage. We even painted the church so it was perfect, and we had opera singers at our reception singing beautifully as guests mingled. But as I was walking down the aisle, I knew full well I was making a huge mistake. But I was already tied to this man by having his child; it just felt like the next thing to do. Some silly part of me thought, *He may treat me better if I'm his wife.*

Kevin never wore his wedding ring. He said it dated back to when he was a builder and was afraid it would get caught in machinery—another story I believed. I think our elaborate wedding was a band-aid on a relationship that was digging my grave and burying the person I had once been.

By the time James was four years old, we were living in a mansion—my dream home. It was everything I had ever imagined and more. As soon as we looked at the house, we both fell in love and wanted it: underground wine cellar, a three-car garage to house my sports car and my seven-seater, plus Kevin's vehicle. The seven-million-dollar price tag was more than we could afford, but we were on a trajectory to the stars. It was just another Band-Aid.

Our business portfolio had accumulated properties worth circa $150 million. We were part-owners with three others in a 105-foot superyacht, which was being built in China. Kevin and one of the other boat owners would travel to China once in a while to check on its progress. I had an impressive collection of Louis Vuitton handbags and shoes, and a wardrobe and a jewelry safe to die for. I had a five-carat diamond ring with a D clarity my friends used to call the "Intimidator" (or should I say so-called friends).

Most of our property portfolio was in Christchurch and Kevin was gone from about Tuesday to Friday each week. Then it was Tuesday through Sunday. Eventually, he was gone for weeks at a time. On one weekend, I was visiting a friend's farm and was due to go back on Friday to meet Kevin, who was to be coming back from Christchurch. He told me he couldn't get back because the flights were all booked. But I went online to check, and there were plenty of flights available—just a few of the lies he was getting careless about. I called him back to confront him, and he stopped answering my phone for the entire weekend. I was left feeling lost and alone, and not understanding why. I always believed his excuses. The alternative was too huge and stressful to consider.

Cycle of Abuse

Every time Kevin did something abusive, disrespectful, or violent, apologies and gifts followed ... and every time, I forgave him. Then there would be a gentle, downhill slide to another event—rinse-and-repeat. Except every new event got ever so slightly worse. Often what happens in abusive relationships like this one is that things go from anger and lashing out verbally, and build up over the years to violence and lashing out physically

Many, many things unraveled. Kevin wanted to buy a vineyard. I was dead against it, but he bought it anyway. He'd been having an affair with a person connected to the vineyard and he'd wanted to impress her—it had nothing to do with the life we were creating. That vineyard dragged our portfolio down and sunk it.

One year, on Valentine's Day, I flew to Christchurch to surprise Kevin. Something was not right—from me trying to check into his hotel room, to the manager trying to block me, to meeting Kevin later that night. I joked with the manager, saying, "Ha ha. Are you worried he's having an affair?" Then I thought, *Oh my god, what if he is?* I'll never forget the look on Kevin's face when I walked into the bar where he was sitting with our staff—he wasn't surprised and happy to see me—and it was a look of shock and horror. That night, he was texting on his phone under the table all night, while I tried to have dinner with him and make conversation. (About eighteen months later, when it all blew up, I checked his phone records and confirmed what I was thinking—he was having an affair.)

During that same trip, on Sunday morning, I picked up the local paper and read the gossip column, "About Town." It had a photo page and showcased the week's events. My stomach fell on the floor … there was a photo of Kevin at a black-tie charity dinner—with another woman. He wasn't even trying to hide it. Of course, he had an explanation: who she was, why she was there, that the photographer had snapped them together, not realizing that the woman wasn't his wife. I believed his lies. I didn't want to believe what was right in front of me. *We have a little boy. If what I think is happening is happening, it will destroy our family.*

At one point, I even tried to get myself established in Christchurch, enrolling James in childcare, so I could come down and spend time with Kevin. Living in two cities with a little boy was stressful … and my move to Christchurch ended up being one more nail in my coffin.

The last straw happened. I had a dinner party at home with a few of the local Who's Who. I was in the kitchen helping the caterer prepare the meal, and a text message came into my phone. I picked it up and read, "I'm in bed thinking about you and missing you so much. Love you so much, Cheryl."

I couldn't breathe. It was Kevin's phone, not mine. I confronted him. I had an absolute out-of-body experience. Without regard for the la-di-da people in my formal dining room, I threw a massive mental at him. All the weird little lies and strange instances boiled over. I knew with all my heart that he was living a double life.

Our guests excused themselves and went home. Somehow, my smarts kicked in and I got my thinking under control. *Kevin has consumed a large amount of red wine. No good is going to come of this if I carry on.* Knowing what Kevin was capable of, I was well afraid of mine and James' well-being. So, I diffused the situation, and we went to bed. He was soon snoring off his Pinot Noir, and I snuck out of the house. I drove downtown to the office, pulled out phone records from the Valentine's Day dinner. The "Love you so much" text number that had come that night matched the number he'd been texting under the table on Valentine's Day in Christchurch. So, this affair had been going on for over eighteen months. Yep, it was the woman in the "About Town" column, and yep … Kevin had made a very public fool of me.

They say that when a woman leaves a relationship, it's been going downhill for over two years. They also say that the opposite of love is not hate. If you hate someone, then really, you still love them. So, the opposite of love is neutral. I wasn't neutral. I hated him. I was devastated, betrayed, and hurt. But somehow, I went into self-preservation mode. I had James to think about. I left the office, went home, snuck into bed, and fell asleep.

Over the next days and weeks, I swung between having a leaving strategy and melting down. *How am I going to get out of this toxic situation, raise my son, and get on with my life? Do I have the energy to start all over again?* At some point, it got too hard. I tried to put everything back together, tried to convince myself that Kevin had changed. But too much water had gone under the bridge. I knew this man was bad for me—in fact, I knew this man was bad, full stop. I was having treatment for health-related problems associated with stress and anxiety. An acupuncturist told me my pulse was so faint that my body was like a car I wasn't driving … instead, I was outside of it, on a hill, trying to push it up the hill, exhausted. He was right. I was shattered.

At its worst, Kevin's violence escalated to him kicking me while I was curled up in a ball on the ground, lying on top of James, trying to protect us both. He was arrested for "male assaults female." My body was covered in scratches and bruises, which the police photographed. I wasn't strong enough to go through with the charges, though, and somehow, Kevin manipulated me into dropping them.

Another revolting scenario I will never forget is when the police arrived at our house and took James away from me. I've never felt this low. How could the police take my boy when Kevin was the violent one? At that point, I felt like there was no one on my side. I was alone. I couldn't trust a single soul except myself. That was the last straw.

Kevin and I went into couple's therapy. From my point of view, the therapy wasn't to repair our relationship; it was to help me end it. After many sessions, one of our counselors helped me end the relationship. He asked us both to leave the room, and he brought us back in, one at a time, to ask us if we wanted to stay in the relationship or leave it. Kevin said he wanted to stay, and I said I wanted to leave. So, he informed Kevin that it was over, that he needed to respect my wishes and we needed to draw up a separation agreement. What a relief.

But that was not the end.

I left our home and moved into an apartment with James. It was hard. I left behind everything I'd worked for (for the last seven years). Everything Kevin and I had created was as much mine as it was his, and I walked away. I'd worked right through my pregnancy for our property company, and while James was a baby, I'd rocked him in his cradle under my desk. Most moms slept when their babies slept to recharge batteries and refill their tanks—not me. I worked and worked and worked. I'd had mastitis four times: trying to breastfeed James for a year while under stress was incredibly difficult. I mourned that I couldn't be a more hands-on momma to my boy because of all the hard work I'd put in. To this day, I still suffer from working mom's guilt.

The big house was sold. I was gutted. My family was broken, even my stepdaughters were no longer mine.

With my business eaten up by the property company, I had lost my independence and my source of income. Kevin froze me out. I got no drawings from the company. He stopped paying my rent, my car payments, my credit card—everything. But I was determined to survive. I sold my five-carat diamond (jewelry was not matrimonial property) and lived on that for a while. About the time we had to move out of the big house, a huge amount of my jewelry was stolen. Kevin blamed the movers or cleaners. Would you believe it—twelve years later, a friend Kevin had fallen out with told me that Kevin had taken it. So, not only did he cut off all my money, but he also took the one thing that was outside of matrimonial property: my jewelry.

I fought Kevin legally for three years, trying to get half of what was mine. But the legal fees were crippling and devoured the money from the sale of my ring. I even paid my barrister with the jewelry I had left. I stopped the fight, as I had more important things to focus on, like paying mine and James' living expenses. I learned it didn't matter if you were legally entitled to fifty percent of your wealth. If your ex-husband wants to avoid paying you, he can drag a lawsuit out for years until you give up. So many people over the years said to me things like, "But you were married—how could he not pay you your half?" My reply was, "You assume that the person wanted to do the right thing, which Kevin did not." So, I gave up the legal battle. He won. I learned a few years later that he hadn't even been paying James' school fees, and that if I didn't pay them, James would be kicked out of school. So, I paid the arrears and I continued paying the school fees to this day. What a guy!

Moving On

Remember the story I told you earlier about me and my girlfriend, sitting in my mansion home on that last day, writing a list to "Manifest a Man"? Meeting my Mark saved my life. Not only did he put a roof over our heads, but he also put up with years of Kevin's horrific financial blackmail. I was flat broke from trying to get what was mine. I was at the end of my rope, my health was suffering, my panic attacks were debilitating. I needed to get well and be a mom to James and a partner to this beautiful new heaven-sent man in my life. He did not deserve to be in a relationship with a woman whose ex-husband was still torturing her financially, mentally, and emotionally.

So, with the heaviest of hearts, I trudged into the official assignee's office and declared myself bankrupt. I could not put up with another day of my ex refusing to pay for my car payments or my credit card, or to give me any child support other than the country's minimal amount of $75 per month. I was done. Kevin had taken all of our assets—our finances, our art, most of our household furniture, most of my jewelry, our portfolio. He'd put me in the ground financially, physically, and emotionally. It's a hard thing to be honest and tell the truth about bankruptcy. Despite nothing in this being my fault, I felt like a failure to the nth degree. I'd had an impeccable career in law, but I was so down and out that I was now "the B word"—*Bankrupt*. The only thing that saved a minute amount of my self-esteem was that the creditors that suffered from my bankruptcy were banks, not small businesses.

My life as I knew it was over. I had poured my blood, sweat, and tears into our property company. Our staff and consultants were our family, my office was my happy place, and my days had been filled with the busy running of our portfolio. Then, suddenly, nothing. Everything was gone. I even got served a trespass notice one day when I wanted to pop into the office so James could use the bathroom. My staff refused to open the door. One of them came downstairs and handed me the notice. We were extradited, cut off, shut down, discarded like an old broken toy. It reminded me of that day when the little girl had snapped at me for patting her dogs. *Humanity is cruel.* I was heartbroken. People who had been my family had sided 100 percent with Kevin—because he held the purse strings. It was the epitome of true colors.

I had gone from Rags to Riches to Rags. It was even too much for my gorgeous new Mark, who needed, for his own sanity, to have a break. We separated, which would be the first of a few times we broke up, missed each other, tried again, only to break up again. It was so unfair that both my past and Kevin were still affecting my happiness. So, yep, now not only was I broke, I was alone. Rock bottom doesn't describe how I felt … not to mention the guilt I felt for allowing another man to leave James' life. I was at ground zero, baby, over and out in every way possible.

Chapter Seven:

Going from Rags to Riches

Rinsing and Repeating

Not only was I at rock bottom, but I was also disappointed for putting myself through the last seven years of what now felt like hell. I'd come back to NZ from the UK fit and healthy, physically and mentally. I'd opened to my spiritual side, and learned to manifest the most magnificent wealth into my life at the expense of myself and my self-love. I didn't feel any self-love, just self-pity. *What went wrong? Why did this happen to me?*

At first, I felt like I'd made the wrong decision—at the fork in the road, I'd turned right instead of left. Left to spirituality, right to riches. But then it became clear—Jojo was right when she'd told me there's a lesson at the end of any path we choose. If I hadn't gone through the last seven years, I wouldn't have realized so many of the valuable lessons that have shaped who I am today. "Pressure makes diamonds" became my new motto.

If I hadn't taken that fork in the road, I wouldn't have met Mark. Even though we were not together, I knew he was the one. I wanted him back in our lives. I needed to manifest him back in a way that would benefit his life as well. I needed to learn from the lessons the universe had sent me and get back on track. Back on track to me meant being happy and having a healthy well-being. But, of course, it was not just for me—it was for me and my little boy.

Panic Attacks Tool Kit

I had gotten to a point again where my panic attacks were just so boring. I was over them. They would leave me shattered and physically and emotionally exhausted. "Seriously?" I'd ask myself, "you're going to have a panic attack now? Rack off." So, I got mad at them and slowly, they diminished. I was becoming the boss of me, not them. I'd had enough. They did not serve me in the slightest.

I began developing a toolbox for dealing with my panic attacks. For me, it felt like a survival kit. Looking back on the clean living I'd been doing in the UK, I realized that with no drinking, my physical body was in better shape, and so was my mind. By this time in my life, I'd been suffering panic attacks for nearly twenty years. That takes a toll on a person. I could write an entire book on panic attacks and how to delete them from your life. I'm now fifty years old and haven't had a full-blown panic attack for years. Below are some simple techniques I have developed for helping with anxiety.

Rags to Riches Tip – Manage Rising Panic

Write your own toolbox—list your tools as bullet points. Print it out, laminate it, and keep it in your wallet or handbag, along with your positive affirmations. When you feel the panic rising, the fact that you will switch your brain to finding your toolbox will interrupt the panic attack.

When you feel the warmth of the panic rising…

- *Switch your mind to finding your toolbox or bag of tricks.*
- *Grab some Rescue Remedy [14] and spray it under your tongue.*
- *Interrupt the panic attack by flipping your mind to something else.*
- *Have your toolbox of interrupters ready when you know*

---

[14] Dr. Bach's "Rescue Remedy" is a homeopathic flower essence remedy for shock and panic. You can find it in the form of tincture, spray, lozenge, or cream in the wellness department of your local health food store or naturopathic pharmacy. *Bach Rescue: Original Flower Remedies* (website), "Rescue Remedy," A Nelson & Co Ltd, Updated July 7, 2022, https://www.rescueremedy.com/en-us/.

something will trigger an attack. For me, it was flying. I always have some work or writing ready to do so I can flip my mind on to that instead of thinking about the panic attack.

- *Write a goals list or dream chart of positive things to think about, to help you snap out of it.*
- *Breathe longer out than in. Start breathing out for eight seconds and in for four seconds.*
- *Remember, if in doubt, breathe out.*
- *Start reading something that will switch your mind to something else. I love trashy magazines that don't require any thought. I just look at the beautiful fashion pictures and daydream to get my mind sidetracked.*
- *Start writing something that takes your mind off it. I do emails or something I have prepared that I know I need to do.*
- *Get mad at the panic attack and tell it to bugger off. Say "I don't need you right now. I'm safe. I don't need a fight-or-flight reaction."*
- *Say to yourself, "Are you kidding me? A panic attack right now? Nope —get lost. I'm having too much fun. I can't be bothered with you right now."*
- *Acknowledge it—"Hi, panic. Here you are. But I don't need you right now, so all is well. Bye bye."*
- *Make a joke … "Are you kidding? I'm not running away from a bear, I'm just on a plane."*
- *Affirm—"I'm in charge of my thoughts and my life. I*

choose to be happy and relaxed."

- *Write a huge gratitude list.*
- *I have prescribed medication with me (which I never take, but it helps me to know I have it). The worry about stopping the attack is gone because I know I can take this drug if I get desperate. It will knock me out and the panic will be gone. It has never gotten to a point where I have needed to take it. I can barely read the label of the drugs' bottle, it's so old, but it's a psychological comfort to have them with me.*

These are things that work for me. You may have worked out different techniques that serve you better. There is no one-size-fits-all. The list above is just mine. Write yours down. Even just having the list written and ready to go gives you a sense of comfort that you are prepared and in charge should a panic attack come up. You are in control and on your front foot, not your back foot.

I remember when Jane, a friend of mine, told me she couldn't understand how I could panic on a plane. It was her favorite thing in the world. Jane and Steven would hop on a plane and Jane said it was like stepping into date night. I loved this. They treated flying like their special time together and would sip champagne, chat, and giggle like they were on a date. This has always resonated with me and it is now another thing I think about when we fly. I try to do the same with my special man. It works.

Anxiety and panic are a part of my life. They are part of everyone's life, but some of us have heightened fight-or-flight triggers. For whatever reason—whether I have a predisposition to panic or whether my brother suffocating me triggered it—it's there. As I noted earlier, when I suffered that first huge panic attack, I was terrified—I thought I was going to die. It left me with post-traumatic stress disorder. Now, my fight-or-flight radar is hypersensitive. Acknowledging that this is who I am took a lot of the stress out of it for me. Still, with what had transpired over the last seven years of my life, I needed my anti-panic toolbox more than ever.

Re-Building the Real Me

One thing I'm grateful for is that many people who had known me a long time said that my rags to riches story never changed me as a person. I'd lived a wealthy lifestyle with Kevin, but when it was all gone, I was the same person—I was always kind. I never put myself on a pedestal or behaved differently just because we had money and lived a certain way. There were many instances where I loved contributing and giving to others less fortunate than us. I encouraged Kevin to be generous too, urging him to buy the mother of his girls a new car so she and her girls would be safe driving around town.

So, here I was, eighty-five kilograms (187 pounds) again, suffering panic attacks, on antidepressants, jobless, penniless, single, and a solo mom. James was about to start school and I got myself together enough to realize that any kind of negative talk around him relating to his father would damage him. A therapist told me that talking badly about your child's dad was like pouring acid on his soul. I got the message. I was determined that my dreadful situation would not harm my boy. I went into overdrive to protect him. As I mentioned earlier, the only money Kevin contributed was his private school fees (or so I thought), so I knew James would need to go to a nice local school.

In the first phase of our separation, I didn't stop Kevin from seeing James. In fact, I didn't stand in the way at all. (I will go into this in more detail later.) I was determined to not make my issues with Kevin, James' issues. Kevin was still his dad, and our little boy needed his dad.

At no stage did I apply for a government assistance benefit. I thought that if I had to do that, that would be the last straw. Even my poor little Mom had more money than I did. While I was married, Dad had passed away, and we had sold Mom's house and put her few hundred thousand into the bank so she could live off that and enjoy not having to worry about paying for a home. Kevin and I had put Mom up in a lovely little sunny unit. She was close by; we looked after her, and she used to babysit James. But when I was out on the street, so was Mom.

By this time, I had gone from a 650 m² home to a 95 m² (6996.5 ft² to a 1022.5 ft²) little rental house. Mom moved in with me and helped me with James. Mom was suffering all the usual illnesses and struggles of a person in their seventies, with the added complication that she only had one lung. Mom was an amazing woman, and like me, she rolled with the punches and got on with life, not expecting anything from anyone. She would have given the shirt off her back to help a stranger. I could not have gotten through this time without her. In the middle of the night, when I was having panic attacks, she would lie on the sofa opposite me and just be there. Just before she passed away some years later, I said to her, "Mom, how will I ever cope without you?"

"Darling," she said, "I'm seventy-eight and I still miss my Mom."

With all my might, I rebuilt my life, one brick at a time. The first thing was to get back into a routine of going to an office. I had a great friend who had been there for me during the whole dramatic demise of my marriage. She owned several magazines, and she hired me to sell advertising. She was my lifesaver. She gave me a purpose to get up in the morning and she invited me to many of the magazines' wonderful social engagements. In the months that followed, I made little money. Mom would advance me money from her savings, and I'd pay her back when I made money. I was managing. I didn't love selling advertising, but I became her top salesperson right away and I knew I could sell anything to anyone if I believed in the product.

Another wonderful friend of mine, whom I'd met because our sons went to kindergarten together, was also a guardian angel. During my marriage, the two of us would walk every day, natter about life, and sort out all our problems. I was never honest with her about how bad my life was with Kevin, but it was an escape for me when we were out together walking. We did this for years and she kept me sane during the toughest of days.

She wanted to buy her neighbor's property but was concerned that if the neighbor found out she was the buyer, they would try to make her pay over the top for it. She asked me to go to the auction and bid on the house for her.

I'll never forget this event. It was so funny. I played a super psychological game, turning up in my designer gear, with the one (huge) designer handbag that I had left (by this time I'd sold most of my bags to get money to live on). My bidding style was to be quick and determined, never pausing before placing a bid and giving the other bidders little time to consider their next bid. This gave the others the impression I meant business. Others in the room gave up, thinking that I would never give up, that I would fight to the bitter end. Of course, I had a budget, but they didn't know that. So, we secured the property for my friend at a price she was thrilled about. Later, she handed me a little envelope of cash to thank me. I was embarrassed, but she knew I needed the money. She said, "You know, you should consider doing your real estate papers and selling houses. You would be so good at It."

When I'd worked as a legal executive and a business development manager at the law firm before I got married, I had sat my real estate papers. The idea had been that I would be the agent for our developer clients, and that would save them a huge amount of money in agent's fees when we were selling their properties off the plans. I never used it in the end because the rules were that you needed to be attached to a real estate firm to activate the license. So, it lapsed. I made some inquiries. The rules and law had changed in relation to getting a real estate diploma, so I was required to re-sit the entire license. I used the money my friend had given to me to enroll in the real estate course.

I guess I was still grasping at straws, trying to continue to live the lifestyle I'd been living—or at least I was struggling to let go of it. When things went pear-shaped and I had no money or means of doing anything, I went into the car dealership that my Audi Q7 and my Audi sports car had come from and burst into tears in the salesperson's office. The salesperson was Mark (yes, my Mark!). He was so kind. He told me that both cars were leased and that if I wanted to keep either of them, I'd have huge lease fees to pay. Kevin had been clear: He wasn't paying for them unless I went home to him. So, both vehicles were given back to the dealership and Mark fixed me up with a little Audi A3 that I could afford on the minimal commission I was making from the magazine.

So, with my new real estate license, and still wanting to hold my head up high and keep some kind of self-respect, I headed to a fancy boutique real estate agency to ask for a job. I was well known as an A-lister around town and had been in social pages in the *NZ Herald* most weekends for a few years. So, the owner of the company thought that with my old connections, I would do well. He wasn't wrong. Within a few weeks, I was matching people to properties and moving them around like jigsaw puzzle pieces. I was making new connections and using all my previous legal and sales skills to plow ahead. I had no choice but to make a success out of this.

Real estate is a sport here in New Zealand—everyone lives it and loves to talk about it. We eat, breathe, and sleep rugby and property in this country. So, it throws you into the limelight and the spotlight, if you are any good at it.

I remember the day I put an Open Home flag up outside the first home I had for sale. I thought I was going to die of embarrassment. I crept up the driveway of the home. I looked left and right (to make sure no one I knew was driving down the road), popped the flag up, and scurried back down the driveway into my open house. Yes, from seven years of materialistic, inauthentic yuck, I had baggage I needed to dissolve. I needed to make peace with my new job, my new status, and what I needed to do to earn money again. My poor brain and soul had been scrambled for years by my gaslighting ex-husband—I still had massive low self-esteem and issues of unworthiness. Once again, I had to make peace with having nothing and not worrying about what people thought about me

Rags to Riches Tip – Be Honest with Yourself

What is something you still feel uncomfortable about (even though you know it's not your fault ... it just happened to you, or you found yourself in those circumstances), but even now you struggle to be honest that it happened? It's hard to face trauma, as it's often attached to shame.

For example, I don't want to be honest about growing up in a tiny little house (even though it wasn't my fault—or even anyone's fault). But it's something I struggled to be honest about for years, thinking even as an adult that other people were judging me and thought less of me because of it. It was the shame of those feelings that stopped me from being able to communicate with them or even be honest with myself.

Try writing three columns in your journal. Make the first heading Trauma, the second Feeling, and the third Reaction. For example, your trauma may have been watching your parents' divorce. The associated feeling may have been guilt, or perhaps you felt you were to blame. Your reaction may be to run away from relationships yourself. Sometimes listing your trauma and reactions shows an emerging pattern of what you are ashamed of in your life—and what you are running from.

Trauma Event – How do I feel about it? – How do I react to it?

Notice patterns of what triggers you, how you feel, and your reaction to it or how you try to run and hide from it. There may be some obvious similarities with which you can identify. Then you can bring them to the surface and work on them.

I learned a lot working in this boutique real estate business, but it ended quickly. All I will say is that I learned "how not to do real estate." Some of our values (which related to the way our customers were treated) were out of alignment. I needed to move to another company that fit better—one with a kindness approach. I'd been working on a great listing, which was in another suburb, so I met with the female owner of a nearby real estate company on the other side of town. She was inspirational (albeit tough), but I respected her. I joined, listed a property nearby, and was up and away as an independent real estate agent working for a great company.

I was unstoppable. I embraced every "No" I heard, believing that it would bring me closer to a "Yes." I was kind, helpful, provided relevant information to clients, and engaged in every client interaction. I poured out love, attention, and service to everyone who crossed my path. Sometimes, this was tough, and I had to dig deep. For someone whose own cup was on rock-bottom empty, it was hard work. I felt exhausted constantly—it was my normal. Then I'd get home, put my solo mom hat on, and try to be a fun, happy, carefree momma to my boy.

Despite having a great new property listing to sell and a new office to work for, I had started working in an area a long way from home and James' school, and it wasn't an area I wanted to focus on. James' school was becoming a significant source of leads and connections, and I wanted to foster these. I approached another, larger real estate company nearer to my home. It was my first step away from the first two smaller boutique companies I had worked for and was a much bigger brand and infrastructure. Their model was individual franchise areas, so the business owner owned the office, which sat under a big umbrella company. It wasn't long, perhaps a year later, that I was the number one salesperson in the office. A fire had been lit in my belly. I was determined to succeed.

I was standing on my own two feet! Although I'd given up on ever getting what was legally mine from Kevin, I still hoped he might do the right thing by his son. During my early periods of financial desperation, I had reached out and asked him to pay for things for James. I hated his responses—which were never a simple "Yes" or "No"—he would try to draw me into some mind game or financial blackmail. So, it felt wonderful to know I didn't need to ask for help again or put myself through a demeaning conversation with Kevin. My best healing was getting on with my life and looking after James 100 percent, without his father. At every opportunity, I would breathe out and let go of a little more of the resentment and hurt from those seven awful years of my life. As far as I knew, Kevin was still going strong, but I had nothing to do with him. I'm sure it got to him that he couldn't blackmail me anymore. I wanted nothing from him. So, his narcissistic ego wasn't being fed—at least not by me.

As things unfolded, I tried to stay in touch with my spiritual side and embrace self-care while juggling the tremendous pressure and time constraints of a top real estate agent. It had been three years since the demise of my dreadful relationship. Professionally, I was back on top. I was out of the shackles of bankruptcy and my divorce was stamped. I never received a cent from any of the matrimonial property. But I was free.

By this time, I had full custody of James. As I noted earlier, Kevin did not try to spend much time with him. I took care of all the financial commitments (though Kevin was (and still is) paying the minimum child support of seventy-five dollars per month, because the government makes him). I won't even get into how wrong this is or how Kevin could get away with this. It brought me so much joy and satisfaction to do it all on my own. Kevin would not get the pleasure of thinking he had ruined my life. In fact, it was the exact opposite. I was on my feet, with a good job, a great home for me, James, and Mom, and I was happy and flourishing. Not only that, my "Manifestation of a Man list" had brought me into contact with someone who fit my list—the gorgeous car dealership principal, Mark.

Mark, who had helped me with my cars, was on my radar. He had been so kind—and I thought he was rather delicious. He matched my manifestation list to a tee and slowly but surely, we started to see each other. This was also tough. We were both broken-winged angels who had lost a lot of trust and faith in humanity for ending up with our lots in life. Mark was forty-one, and I was thirty-seven when our worlds blended for the first time. I had so much love to give and there was so much fun I wanted to have. Mark was my rock. We played and had fun like naughty kids and often joked that there was no adult in our relationship. He was so careful with James and tried not to overstep the mark. I was on guard—any sign of an overstep was met with a meltdown from an over-protective momma. Oh my.

Blending our Families

When mark and I got back together after our first break up, blending our families continued to be an enormous challenge. His two girls were struggling with their parents' separation and found it difficult to accept another woman in their dad's life. James was too young to create any major issues, but the biggest challenge was my overriding desperation to protect him. If there was any sign of conflict or stress in his direction, I would throw myself on top of it, overreacting to save him. This could have been anything, from ordering his food at a restaurant, to Mark asking him to pick up a toy. To make things a little more challenging for me to chill out, as I mentioned earlier, James was very asthmatic, and he had anaphylaxis to nuts. These were both scary medical issues that could have ended his life if I didn't care for and supervise him. So, I was hypervigilant when it came to protecting him—from things that might trigger his asthma, to things that might contain nuts, to … well, everything. My anxiety morphed into hypersensitivity. He'd witnessed and been around too many things that no little person should ever have had to see. I didn't want him to see another thing that could hurt him. Of course, I was making a rod for my own back. By over-protecting James in every situation, I was taking his soul journey and his right to make his own decisions away. He couldn't even order from a menu; I'd be jumping in to suggest all the things he loves (that didn't have nuts).

Sending James off to stay with Kevin was stressful—I was hoping and praying he wouldn't have an asthma attack or come in contact with nuts. My trust in Kevin's ability to look after him was not strong. When Kevin and I separated, I didn't stop him from having access to James. I knew that while he had been violent to me, he had never laid a hand on James directly—albeit he had behaved badly around him. I had witnessed other mothers who had prevented their children from seeing their dads for no good reason. Even though I had a good reason, I weighed up what would be more damaging to my son, not seeing his father or seeing his imperfect father. So, I thought, *Trust the universe, everything will work out.* I agreed to fifty percent custody, and we shared our boy. I hated it when I had to say goodbye to James and send him to his dad's. I felt sick and panicky and didn't sleep well from the time he left to be with Kevin until he came home. It was hard for me, but I held on to the fact that it had to be what was right for James. He was a boy and needed his father—or that's what I thought. In the end, I resolved to let James decide, and that I would monitor things.

As Kevin went on with his life and bounced from one toxic relationship to another, so did James. He met all Kevin's women friends. The most volatile relationship Kevin had (and likely this woman had a worse time of it than I did), was with a lady he later married. I'm not sure who was more toxic, him or her, but they had a tumultuous, horrific relationship that resulted in James coming home from his dad's telling all kinds of stories, including one where security met them at the airport when their plane landed. That relationship ended in divorce. It's challenging with children to listen to their stories and read between the lines without over- or under-reacting. I felt like I was between a rock and a hard place. Do I continue to let him see his dad or not? Are these stories damaging to him or not? He didn't seem upset. But he'd recount the stories, and I'd think, *This can't be good for a child ... to talk about violence, alcoholic behavior, chairs being thrown out of windows, trips to hospital to treat injuries, and so on. This cannot become his normal.* The worst thing was that James often sided with his father, blaming Kevin's partner. Hmmm.

I wanted to get full custody of James, but I knew how hard Kevin would fight me for him, and I didn't want to stress James out more than he already was with another court battle. Luckily, the

Children, Young Person Family Society (CYPFS) took the decision out of my hands. A CYPFS representative rang me saying, "Put it this way, Heather, if you don't apply for full custody, we will have you for neglect."

"Perfect," I said. So, I applied to the court and was given 100 percent custody of James. The universe and karma had sorted it all out for me. From that day on, James didn't see Kevin. Maybe once a year at Christmas, but even then, Kevin skipped the odd Christmas, depending on his social life, and if he was in Auckland or not.

So, Kevin put very little effort into parenting and made a negligible financial contribution. I dearly hope James never takes his father's neglect as a reflection of him. Kevin has missed out on the most wonderful boy and the fun of raising such a neat kiddo. I'm so blessed to have James and am grateful to Kevin for making that part of my life 100 percent perfect (by encouraging me to have a child).

So, Mark and I had James full time, and it was only fair that Mark should be able to behave as his parent, given that we were his parents now, 100 percent of the time. But I was overprotective. If Mark asked James to do anything or help with anything, I would jump down his throat. In hindsight, I was ridiculous. But at the time, it was all I knew. It frustrated me that I had such a lot of baggage and damage from my relationship with Kevin.

For Mark and me to create a healthy, beautiful relationship with what we both already had going on in our lives was an enormous challenge. We both so deserved to be loved and to have each other to love. I wanted to be with him, but his girls were not accepting of us, and Mark was getting sick of me being overprotective of James. So, we did a dance of breaking up, missing each other desperately, me promising to change, and getting back together. All the while, I was working seven days a week selling houses and juggling looking after James with the help of my elderly mother (thank God for Mom).

Learning to Trust Again

Despite the success that came from working hard in real estate, it all seemed pointless without my family and my Mark by my side. I knew that together, we could achieve anything. Our longest break up was a year apart, and I'd done a lot of personal growth and soul searching. It was a challenging year, and James and I missed Mark. We didn't want to take him for granted ever again, and in that year, we learned more than ever that relationships take work. It was hard for me to learn to trust again—to trust that everything Mark did was not out to get me or designed to cheat me out of everything and take it all for himself. Just when I thought Mark had really moved on without us, he came back. Our crazy blended family became our family and home was in each other's arms, no matter where we were at or what we were doing. His girls had seen their dad sad without me, and they were old enough to understand and want him to be happy. We joke nowadays that when we travel internationally, we are a travel agent's nightmare—five of us, with four different surnames. It's complicated!

Telling myself that everything happens for a reason, that it was all part of the universe's Big Plan for me, required me to dig deep. I couldn't believe that the universe had put all of this in place for me to learn from and change—what a massive, exhausting, almost life-ending lesson! It all led me to one of my favorite sayings: "Diamonds are made under immense pressure." It's true. I'm such a massive achiever and manifester that without a huge amount of stress, I would not have come so far or been able to dig in to do what was required for the ten years that lay ahead ... so I could get to The Real Me

Chapter Eight:

Finding the Real Me

Starting Again and Making a Go of It

My first year in real estate, I earned about $150,000 in gross commissions, which converted to about half that by the time taxes and fees were taken out. It was about the same salary as a legal executive salary and enough for me to pay for my car, rent, and child expenses … you get the picture. I tossed up going back to a law firm and working nine-to-five, but I needed to pick James up from school. Seven days a week, I juggled his school hours and got the help I needed with him. My mom had been amazing, but we managed to find a solution which would give Mom her own place again. We found her a tiny leasehold flat in an okay suburb close to us. We budgeted so that the costs would be affordable for about seven years before she ran out of money. So, we took a risk and Mom was happy enough being back in her own home—and back to humble beginnings.

I then arranged for an au pair from overseas to come and live with James and me, a young man named Jens from Germany. Au pairs were affordable because, mostly, they need a place to live and to be looked after while experiencing a new country. So, the wages were low, and we provided accommodation and food. Jens was fabulous. He was like a big brother to James and because he was getting overseas work experience; it was affordable child support. Having a live-in au pair was a lifesaver when James was little and I was getting back on my feet. I didn't have to drop what I was doing and pick him up from school and Jens played wonderful boy games with him, which James loved.

Having Jens support me gave me so much more freedom and time to put into my relationship with Mark—and thank goodness, we put love first and tried to make a go of it. Jens loved Mark too, and somehow, we and our crazy little family situation got back on track. Juggling our blended family was an ongoing challenge and James was now very much our son. The girls were going through their teenage years and Mark was trying to figure out how he could fit in to their lives now that he wasn't living with them and they were living at the opposite end of Auckland. He would try to have dinner with them once a week or meet them for coffee. I used to think how amazing his children were. They were raised differently from James; they were grateful for everything they were given. Not only that, they seemed to breeze through their teens. I know their mom bore the brunt of it as they lived with her full time, but they were such good girls and were committed to doing well and being independent. James was spoiled and protected, and he got anything pretty much he wanted from me— as long as I could afford it. There were still times when I tried to rescue James from Mark trying to parent him. Again, I see now that my behavior was absurd—grounded in mistrust and fear.

But over time, I let go of my fear of James being traumatized by a father-figure, and trusted that Mark would always do his best by James and me—and he did. In the end, I realized I could not be with Mark until I let go of the mistrust that had been cultivated in me after Kevin's massive betrayal. I did the growing I needed to do, and the rest is well ... one fantastic happy ending (or should I say beginning).

It's hard to describe the grit and determination I had to do what I did. I had to call on every inch of my being and stay focused. I wrote daily goals lists, meditated morning and night, and chanted affirmations: "Every day, in every way, my life gets better and better" and "I have financial abundance now." I chanted them repeatedly—these affirmations were imprinted on my brain. I wanted a good life for me and James, and I was determined to get it.

Every cent I earned from selling properties in those early days went into paying to live, and paying legal fees for my matrimonial legal battle. That's when it got to a point where I threw in the towel and let go of trying to get half of what I had created and start again. Mark used to say to me, "Honey, let's just start this relationship from zero. Let's just start again." It was one of the hardest things I've ever done, letting go of the past and everything I'd worked for. The biggest challenge for me was letting go of the resentment I felt for all the time I'd put into our business instead of watching James grow up. He was at school now and those important early years were gone. But that was all in the past, and Mark was right—we needed to begin at the beginning. We were determined to make a go of it—and we did!

Spread a Little Love Around

You never really stop working on a healthy, happy relationship. It's a thing you need to do daily. Every day is a new day, with a new challenge, not only for you, but for your partner. Every day, work on whatever is placed in front of you and tackle it with love and kindness. With all your might, you need to come from a place of love, not fear. Fear will eat you alive and create unrest and unhappy results. Coming from love will do the opposite, even though you may need to look well within yourself to find it. Try thinking about the opposite of negative. Every time a negative comes to mind, think of the positive that represents love.

Rags to Riches Tip – Spread a Little Love Around

This is a great exercise to do when you are immersed in your own self. Step outside of that and be kind, loving, and caring towards someone else. I've learned it's one of the best self-healing exercises you can do.

- *Sometimes, the best thing we can give away is our time to someone else who needs it.*
- *Bring an assistant or colleague a cup of coffee.*
- *Ask about someone's weekend and what they got up to.*
- *Look for opportunities to donate money, food, clothing, or your time.*
- *Just do something you normally wouldn't do out of pure kindness. Straight away, you'll feel better about yourself and your own situation.*

So, that's my story. I went from selling my "Intimidator" five-carat diamond in order to feed myself and my son, to enduring more pressures, trials, and tribulations than anyone should ever have to endure (and I have the scars to prove it). I emerged a bright, shining star. And now that I have enough money to buy another "Intimidator," the satisfying feeling for me is that I don't need or even want another one. To me, life is all about experiencing the abundance all around us, the beauty and miracles of the world, loving my family and friends, experiencing every minute of every day, and enjoying life in all its divine glory. Still, I look back on my life with wonder—and marvel at how I made it through. I will never forget the journey I've been on, or the people I encountered along the way—some good, some bad. With all of them, lessons were learned. Nothing is ever a waste of time if you learned something from it and changed your life for the better as a result.

As I come to the end of my story, in my haste to get it all out, I realize there's a few pertinent details I didn't share, so stay with me while I recap those here....

Trusting in the Universe
(to Bring Only Good Things)

Mark, James, and I had everything. I couldn't have wished for more in life. Mark and I both wanted to create a better life for ourselves and our families. We both had a desire to be in touch with our spiritual selves and manifest happiness and well-being. Trying to sustain a healthy relationship with what we both faced was challenging. We often used to say that keeping a relationship on track with the added challenges we had was like driving a car on ice at top speed and trying to keep it driving straight.

Mark is a selfless, kind-hearted, loving, incredible human being, whose only desire in life is to love and help me and the people he cares about, often to the detriment of his own health and happiness. The list I wrote to attract my perfect man was detailed in every way. I just needed to get myself sorted to a point where I could be as good for him as he was for me.

Mark was dependable, reliable, and steadfast, and together we were living loving, authentic, normal lives. Having been through what I had, it was so important to me to live my Truth. Sadly, most of my former friends dropped away—I guess they wanted to hang out with the rich developer guy with all the money and influence. I bore no grudges. Later in life, five people came back to apologize (which wasn't necessary and part of their healing, not mine). Kevin had betrayed pretty much everyone who had supported him at the time of our breakup. They came out of the woodwork around the same time. From what I understand, Kevin lost all his money (and a lot of them relied upon him for fees to keep their businesses afloat). The way they had treated me weighed on their consciences, and without the fear of losing Kevin's business, they offered explanations of why they had dumped me and James all those years ago. It was sad—sad that they still thought money alone would bring them happiness, sad that they were just fake friends of ours/Kevin's, and also sad that they had made their decisions based on money, not on what was right or what they believed in. I was polite and understanding— and then I closed the door.

Real estate can bring out the worst in people—it can be a dog-eat-dog environment because the players deal with enormous sums of money and the emotional turmoil of people's lives. I wanted to have a business that was kind, caring, helpful, and loving to its people. So, setting up my own office became a priority. My self-esteem was solid, and I wanted my own business—I'd created my own company with Via Property, and I knew I could do it again. With Mark's support, and with determination, goal setting, focus, and commitment, we made it happen. My very own little real estate company sat under the umbrella of the big mother ship—but it was my franchise, mine to create and mold. I was a business owner once again, and this time I was captain of my ship. My sheer determination and grit had brought me sustainable success.

I saw being the boss of my company as a way of helping and mentoring others—perhaps my success could help others succeed, too. I had an ingrained desire that brought me a huge amount of joy—seeing others succeed made my heart sing. So, I wanted to create some kind of tool kit (like my panic attack tool kit) to help others—especially women who found themselves in a similar situation—to get started again. I spoke at several events about the rise-and-demise and rise-again of my success. I loved inspiring young people to be the best they can be and empowering them to rely on themselves alone to get where they wanted to go. I wanted them to dig deep and know that if, like me, they woke up one day in a terrible situation, they could get out there and start again. I wanted to empower them to build resilience, so they would not have to go through the horrific situation I did to learn that lesson in life.

So, with my success set in concrete, I set sail. The lessons that followed for me were many—and they weren't all happy ones. I learned that not everyone you help will be grateful, not everyone will remember, and some people will even betray you. My heart would sink when someone's ego took over, or they turned on me, or they left me in their wake. I learned to let go of my ego, to do all things with love, and to help others unconditionally, no strings attached. I learned to take joy from others' success and expect nothing in return. After my acrimonious battle with Kevin, I'd learned that bitterness doesn't serve anyone. In fact, it only eats you up and doesn't affect others in the slightest. I had to trust in the universe and know that everything was happening in perfect divine timing and that everything was happening for a reason.

Rags to Riches Tip – Affirm Only Good Things

Another favorite affirmation (or "positive self-talk") of mine is, "Only good things happen to me."

When you believe this, it's not possible to be affected or saddened by what others do or how they behave. This is your journey, no one else's.

If you believe that only good things happen to you, then when something appears to be a "bad thing," how often do you say, "It's just as well that happened, because otherwise, this other thing wouldn't have happened?" For example, maybe you missed out on buying a house you loved, but then another one came along, which was nicer and that you love so much more.

On the front page of your journal, write this affirmation:

"Every day, in every way, my life gets better and better."[15] ... "Only good things happen to me that are for my highest good."

If you can memorize this and say it over and over when you are walking, working out, or driving, it becomes a natural go to self-prayer or affirmation to improve your life on all fronts.

The only thing that mattered to me was being able to sleep at night, with unconditional love for myself and my world. James and Mark have my unconditional love, and they also have my deepest respect, support, and admiration for who they are as people and the success they have achieved both together and individually. They have a special stepdad, stepson relationship and it's better than a lot of father-son relationships I've seen.

Together, we've never been happier. Mark and I got married, combined our families, our homes, and our successful careers. We make it work. We support each other in everything we do. My success is Mark's, and his is mine. It's a partnership in every sense of the word.

---

[15] Émile Coué, Ibid.

A Journey of His Own

Mark's journey to success is a wonderful story to share. He's been with the same company for thirty-two years. His life mirrored mine in many ways—he had started as a young mechanic and worked his way up to being Dealer Principal of a huge luxury car brand. I was so proud of him and loved the fact that he'd come from a similar background to mine. He'd had the grit and determination to get to where he was.

A favorite story he tells is when he walked into the dealership thirty years ago and asked for a job. The owner told him that if he could put the car that lay in a thousand pieces on the floor of the workshop back together, he would give him a job. So, Mark did it. He became an A-grade Porsche mechanic, salesperson, and eventually was running what became the top dealership in the country. Wow, what a story. He is such an inspiration and was so loved and respected by his peers.

After thirty-two years in the same business, Mark wanted and needed a change of job and, over time, he was drawn into my real estate business. Our business won the best New Office award the year we opened and continued to win growth awards and other accolades. Mark handed in his resignation at his job and took the reins of our business full time. It was a massive relief for me—I was spread thin. I was doing the accounts, recruiting, running the office, and selling properties. Mark had so much experience running a big corporation, his input was incredibly valuable. The team loved him. We attracted and kept some great people, and our small business was growing from strength to strength.

Reaching the Pinnacle

In 2016, I reached what I consider the pinnacle of my real estate career. At the annual Ray White recognition awards ceremony, they count down from the top twenty agents in the country to number one. It was getting to about number five and my heart was sinking: *"Oh, no, I've missed out."* Typical self-doubt. *Oh, my goodness, I didn't even make the top twenty. How can that be?* So, when they announced that "The No. 1 Salesperson in the country for this year is ... Heather Walton," I almost fell off my chair. It was a night to remember. I was getting recognition for everything I'd worked so hard for. Seven years ago, I was a penniless solo mom, and here I was, the top agent out of 1,700 other salespeople in the country within our network. I won the overall Supreme Award (which included the residential, commercial, and rural sectors combined), Top Marketer, and No. 1 in Growth. It was huge—I'd won everything there was to win. If that wasn't the universe telling me I'd made it, I don't know what would be. I breathed a tremendous sigh of relief. I'd done it.

James was so proud of me. He knew how hard I'd worked and what I'd sacrificed to get the life that we wanted, to live where I wanted us to live, and to have what I wanted us to have. It went without saying, of course, that I could not have achieved all of this without Mark's support. He'd been such a great dad to our son and the girls and a fantastic boss to our staff. He was—and is—my absolute rock.

Mark and I both want to live in a beautiful home we can be proud of, and we both love renovating houses. We indulged our creative sides and got a lot of personal satisfaction from transforming old, dated homes to better versions of themselves—a bit like we'd done for ourselves. It was like satisfying my inner child repeatedly. Make a home beautiful … rinse, repeat. Inching ahead … buying, renovating, selling … was a way for us to get ahead, recreate some wealth, and plan for our future. We both believe that "only good things happen to us," and we manifest those good things by making our dream board a routine part of our lives. At first, we started with pictures of things we wanted, and we kept the collage we created on our computer wallpaper or glued images into our journal. We became faster and faster at ticking off our goals and lists of things we wanted to achieve. One outstanding achievement was manifesting a huge waterfront property on the beach—it was amazing to acknowledge that it was far better than the "mansion" I had to move out of when I broke up with Kevin. We had ended up with a waterfront penthouse in Queenstown, a reserve waterfront property at Omaha, our clifftop home on the beach, plus our now-significant rental portfolio, businesses, vehicles, and boat. Our children all have lovely lives, went to excellent schools, studied at great universities and, best of all, they didn't experience the hardship that Mark or I did when we were growing up.

The future for Mark and me is bright. We'll keep what we have, we'll enjoy, maintain, and grow our three real estate offices, we'll provide mentoring and support for our team, and we'll live the life that we worked so hard to create. We are so grateful for everything we have, and we've put some daily rituals into practice for the immense gratitude we feel. These are listed in the chapter below. I hope you have fun manifesting your own miracle life story! But remember no pain, no gain. Here is a wonderful but challenging tip to help you make immediate and life changing routines for sustainable long-term growth in all areas of your life.

Real Me Action – Joining the 5:00 a.m. Club

Rising an hour before you need to can give you a head start on your day. This hour should be split into three twenty minutes slots:

- *Twenty minutes' intense exercise—we have high intensity interval training (HITT) bikes. You must sweat.*
- *Twenty minutes' reading, writing, journaling, learning. This time can be broken into a section on gratitude; a section about "If today was going to be great, here's what would happen;" and a section where you write or read some positive affirmations to yourself.*
- *Twenty minutes' meditation—get your head and heart set for a wonderful day.*

Try to do the twenty minutes of intense exercise and sweat if you can; as noted, it burns off the previous day's cortisol and helps methylate stress hormones.

The twenty minutes of self-development (journaling, etc.) can be the most important part of your day. Even just writing down your daily gratitude lists and what would make the day a great day for you can really help you grow. This is something you can get your children to do from an early age and they can carry it through their entire lives.

Twenty minutes of meditation can set you up for your day and make you bulletproof, so life can bring on whatever the day offers.

This process IS life changing and integral to your ongoing health and happiness.

Health and Well-being Rituals and Key Points

Remember I told you I once weighed eighty-five kilograms? At the top of the scale, I was ninety-three kilograms (205 pounds). At the height of trying to recreate our riches, Mark ballooned to 120 kilograms (264.5 pounds). Part of our healing journey was to stop thrashing ourselves and implement some self-love and well-being. It had been an intense twelve years (from when I was a flat-broke solo mom, to meeting Mark, to today) and self-love and care had taken a back seat for a lot of this time. When I look back, I see my journey as a marathon, but really it was just taking things one day at a time and putting one foot in front of the other. It's never too late to implement change or to change your routines or rituals. Here are some of my favorites, and they are simple to implement.

Intermittent Fasting

This is a daily part of our lives now. After our 5:00 a.m. Club morning routine, we walk our dog, Cody Bear (a toy American Schnauzer), and get a coffee from our favorite seaside cafe. Black coffee is best as it doesn't trigger metabolism and doesn't break the fast. I look forward to this part of the day. Our clifftop home has a staircase going from the bottom of the garden directly onto the beach. Our beach is tranquil and surrounded by sheer, ragged rock cliffs. We carry our shoes, walking barefoot in the soft white sand as Cody runs around between our legs, chasing birds and begging us to throw the ball. We walk down our stairs onto the sand, and fifteen minutes later, we're at our cafe. I often have "pinch myself moments"—*I can't believe this is really my life.*

Intermittent fasting creates a big gap between two meals to enable your body to process and recuperate from all the eating and drinking we do. It uses up the fuel in your body so you are basically fasting and burning fat. It's done at a very easy time. You finish dinner and don't eat again until a gap of about sixteen hours has transpired. For example, finish dinner at 7:00 p.m. and don't eat again until 11:00 a.m. This is incredibly easy and is the most effective way to lose weight and correct your metabolism with little change or stress.

Rags to Riches Tip – Drink Water

Drinking water is a life-changer. Being dehydrated has a huge amount to do with our health and our moods. I'm not a huge fan of plain water but I get it in other ways. I love sparkling water, I drink water infused with herbal tea bags, and I put effervescent hydration tablets into my water to make it taste better.

I am not staunch about my rituals because I think a lot of them set you up for failure. If you love water, then great, drink between two and three liters a day. If you are like me, try some of my ideas to get more hydration into your body. The weight will drop off and your moods will be so much better.

Mental Health

Over the last twenty years plus, more than once I thought about ending it all. Having my son was one reason I never did and really,

I didn't want to die. I wanted to live my best life and leave behind a legacy that could help other people in my situation. I could write an entire book about mental health and well-being. Panic attacks and anxiety are linked to depression and mental health, and as you know, I am no stranger to panic attacks or anxiety. The anti-depressants I went on and off of for over twenty years were, I think, mainly placebos. But mentally, I thought they would help me cope and not suffer panic attacks, and that was enough to pop me out of the deepest, darkest moments of despair. But I have much better tricks nowadays.

It's so important to realize that our body's health has a direct link to our mental health. There are some incredible Chinese herbs that are more effective than medications and are far better for you. Any good qualified Chinese herbalist can make you up a potion of these little gems. Taken as directed, they will keep you stable, and help you sleep better and feel more relaxed. Other little jewels, like magnesium (to help you relax and sleep) and 5HTP (to help balance hormones), can be real life-changers.

Gut Health

Gut health has a huge amount to do with our moods. Our gut is known as our "second brain." If you crave sugar and eat a lot, you know the addiction. The pull towards eating chocolate (or craving sweets) has been compared to a cocaine addiction. So, it's imperative to crack the addiction to sugar. The less sugar you eat, the less you will crave. It's a vicious cycle. Chinese herbs can help with this. Taking probiotics to balance your tummy flora can help you get your gut health back in balance. Getting your "second brain" healthy will help with your mental health. Of course, there are other ways, too. I try to go to a health retreat annually where I eat only plant-based food for a week, which helps restore a healthy gut and puts me back on track for eating well and honoring my body.

Self-Care and Self-Love

Most of us have spent our lives thrashing ourselves to achieve what we think is a drive to set ourselves up for the future. Often, though, if we pause and examine what we are trying to achieve, we don't even know. It's so important to stop and smell the roses. Give your brain and yourself an opportunity to re-evaluate your path and your goals. Sometimes, doing something as simple as going for a massage or a facial, taking a walk on your own, or taking a hot bath with some bath salts is all you need to put a little gas back in your tank. A favorite saying of mine (like they say on the plane) is that "You need to put your mask on first before you can help others." You are no good to anyone if you don't take care of yourself. We all suffer a bit of guilt when we do something special for ourselves, right? But remember, you owe it to yourself and the people you love to take care of yourself first.

Rags to Riches Tip – Write Down Goals with Gratitude

This is a no compromise activity—which is why it appears in this book more than once. I want this to sink in: Write down what you are grateful for each day and review your goals. This is one of the single most important things you can do towards achieving better health and happiness and creating the life you want. Goals are wonderful because they can be broken down into headings:

- Health goals.
- Wealth and financial goals.
- Personal or relationship goals.

You don't need your goals to be realistic. You can write goals that would blow your mind. If I had been told twelve years ago that I would live in a ten-million-dollar home and have the assets I have now, I wouldn't have believed it was possible—it would have seemed like too high a mountain to climb. So, to make your goals feel more manageable, you can break them down into a timetable: listing three-month, six-month, one-year, or five-year goals.

Rags to Riches Tip – Be Kind

Pause. Give yourself a moment. We are too quick to react to this life. We allow other people to affect our moods and ruin our day. Take back control. When something interferes with the flow of your day, let the situation or another person's words wash over you. Pause. Then, run through a few questions in the flowchart below.

Ask yourself, "Do I need to engage with or respond to this?"

If the answer to the first question is "Yes":

- *If possible, write down your response and review it. Remove the emotion from your response. Make sure your response is kind.*
- *Consider whether you can deliver your response verbally, without getting emotional—or whether it's preferable (or more appropriate) to respond to an email or text without engaging in any negative exchange, delivering only kind facts.*
- *Respond with love, compassion, and kindness. Know that if you do anything else, you become the owner of the negative situation or words to which you are responding.*

If the answer to the first question is "No," ask yourself, "Can I let this go, leaving the harsh event or unkind words with the person who owns them (not me)?"

- *Let it go. Move on with your life.*

Accepting the Real You and Taking Off in Your New Direction

After a lot of much needed self-care and self-love, things took off for me in an unusual way. For most people, "taking off" would mean putting out a huge amount of energy. Your own "taking off" story will depend on where you are at in life. The *Rags to Riches Tips* in this book may set you off on a massive drive to achieve.

But for me, my whole life has already been about achieving. So, after I took the time to give myself self-care, what took off for me? I was at peace. I felt acceptance. I could stop trying, doing, wanting, making everything end in "ing" and just *be*. It was like pulling a blanket of peace up over my entire body and mind and just closing my eyes and breathing out. "It is okay, Heather, you're done. Now, just enjoy. You don't need to keep running on this treadmill of life. You're there."

I couldn't just wake up one day and decide I was done. I needed something in between my whole life up to this point and the next chapter to consolidate my life, my lessons, my own beliefs—the entire lot. So, the last leg of my journey was heading to a health retreat on the South Island of New Zealand called Aroha (which, in Maori, means Love). I went on my own for eight days. I love my own company.

Aroha was just what I needed—a complete pause from my day-to-day life and from my day-to-day people. I could write an entire book on that experience. The week encompassed everything I have written about in this book (so getting to this point in the book feels like the completion of a full circle). The thirteen people who were on that week-long retreat were all there at the right place, at the right time. They were in my life that week for a reason, a season, and some will even remain for a lifetime. The daily routine was flow: the people were in flow, the entire week was in flow.

I left the retreat with a clear vision of what my life had been about and what my future would be about. But mostly, I had a strong sense of knowing that what really mattered was right here, right now, in this moment. I knew what was important to hold on to and what was important to let go of. Everyone in the group even wrote a letter to themselves, which Aroha will post to us in one year from our retreat date. I can't remember what I wrote in my letter to myself, but I'm pretty sure one thing was a promise to write this book.

It's amazing how you can spend your whole life trying, doing, and achieving, and sometimes, all you need is space and time around you to let the fragments of all that *doing* settle and sink into your DNA—so you can simply become, and accept who you are, where you have come from, and where you are going. Yesterday is history, tomorrow is a mystery, and right now is the magic.

The Aroha retreat was the third retreat I've done in this lifetime (the first retreat was my version of "eat, pray, love" in India[16] (a different kind of retreat, but a perfect one at the time), the second retreat was in Australia after the end of my abusive relationship and start of my new happier life (which was also the kick-start for my twenty-five kilo (55 pounds) weight loss journey to release all that emotional baggage I had accumulated), and then this one—Aroha—my third and most enjoyable retreat so far! In Aroha, I felt I was my real self. I enjoyed myself. It was like testing out the "real me" for the first time.

Yep, the Aroha retreat was a massive conclusion to a fifty-year journey for me. My journey started, literally, from me wearing rags, to journeying along a twisting road through trials and triumphs, to riches … to finally, gently arriving at the real me. And boy, am I going to enjoy the next fifty!

Who is the real you? Have you met him/her yet? Don't waste another moment.

---

[16] Shout out to author Elizabeth Gilbert for this perfect description of the self-empowerment journey! Elizabeth Gilbert, *Eat, Pray, Love* […] (New York: Riverhead Books, 2007), https://www.amazon.com/Eat-Pray-Love-Everything-Indonesia/dp/0143038419.

Epilogue:

Consider This Wonderful Teaching by the Buddha[17]

One day, the Buddha and a large following of monks and nuns were passing through a village. The Buddha chose a large shade tree to sit beneath so the group could rest a while out of the heat. He often chose times like these to teach,

[17] Sarah Conover, *Kindness. A Treasury of Buddhist Wisdom for Children and Parents* (Cheney, WA: Eastern Washington University Press, 2001), https://www.amazon.com/Kindness-Treasury-Buddhist-Children-Parents/dp/091005567X.

so he began to speak. Soon, villagers heard about the visiting teacher and many gathered around to hear him.

One surly young man stood to the side, watching as the crowd grew larger and larger. To him, there were too many people traveling from the city to his village, and each had something to sell or teach. Impatient with the bulging crowd of monks and villagers, he shouted at the Buddha, "Go away! You just want to take advantage of us! You teachers come here to say a few pretty words and then ask for food and money!"

But the Buddha was unruffled. He remained calm, exuding loving kindness. He requested politely that the man come forward, and asked, "Young sir, if you purchased a lovely gift for someone, but that person did not accept the gift, to whom does the gift then belong?"

The odd question took the young man by surprise. "I guess the gift would still be mine because I was the one who bought it."

"Exactly so," replied the Buddha. "Now, you have just cursed me and been angry with me. But if I do not accept your curses, if I do not get insulted and angry in return, these curses will fall back upon you—the same as the gift returning to its owner."

The young man clasped his hands together and slowly bowed to the Buddha—he had learned a valuable lesson. The Buddha concluded for all to hear, "As a mirror reflects an object, as a still lake reflects the sky: take care that what you speak or act is for good. For goodness will always cast back goodness and harm will always cast back harm."

Bibliography

Bach Rescue: Original Flower Remedies. "Rescue Remedy." A
Nelson & Co Ltd. Accessed July 12, 2022.
https://www.rescueremedy.com/en-us/.

Bach, Richard. *Jonathan Livingston Seagull.* New York: Scribner,
2006.

Brainy Quotes. "Tracy McMillan Quotes." Brainy Quotes.
Accessed July 10, 2022.
https://www.brainyquote.com/authors/tracy-mcmillan-
quotes.

Conover, Sarah. *Kindness: A Treasury of Buddhist Wisdom for
Children and Parents.* Cheney, WA: Eastern Washington
University Press, 2001.

Furtado, Nelly. "I'm Like a Bird." Track 1 on *Whoa, Nelly!*
DreamWorks, 2000, compact disc.

Gilbert, Elizabeth. *Eat, Pray, Love: One Woman's Search for
Everything Across Italy, India and Indonesia.* New York:
Riverhead Books, 2007.

Goodreads. "Émile Coué > Quotes." Goodreads. July 16, 2022.
https://www.goodreads.com/author/quotes/192066._mile
Cou.

Hay, Louise. *You Can Heal Your Life.* Carlsbad, CA: Hay House Inc, 1984.

Jeffers, Susan. *Feel the Fear and Do It Anyway.* New York: Ballantine Books, 2006.

Kehoe, John. *Money, Success, and You.* Montreal: Zoetic Inc, 1998.

Patton, George S. Jr. Goodreads. July 16, 2022. https://www.goodreads.com/quotes/53033-pressure-makes-diamonds.

Robbins, Anthony. *Unleash the Power Within.* New York: Simon & Schuster, 2020.

Share International. "The Great Invocation." Share International. July 16, 2022. https://www.share-international.org/background/xmission/tm_invocation.htm

Spice Girls. "Wannabe." Recorded December 1995. Track 1 on *Spice.* Virgin, 1996, compact disc.

Heather Walton, "Heather Walton," The Real Me Limited, August 4, 2022. https://www.theheatherwalton.com.

Ziglar, Zig. *How to Be a Winner.* Wheeling, IL: Nightingale Conant Corp., 1990.

Born in 1971, Heather Walton was the fourth child of a family living in rural South Auckland, New Zealand. Like most parents with large families, her mom and dad were exhausted, and by the time Heather came along, she pretty much raised herself. From a young age, Heather learned to overcome adversity, and it soon became her greatest life skill. Growing up in rags, knowing she deserved more in life, Heather began her lifelong quest for success. By consuming self-help books and implementing their advice, she learned to manifest wealth. Quickly. The only problem? She forgot to be happy—so she went from Rags to Riches—and wound up miserable. It was time to clear the decks and start over. Back at zero, Heather was broken, financially, physically, and emotionally. Life had taught her a valuable lesson: Life is not just about surviving; it's about thriving! Heather's memoir is about her journey from Rags to Riches and, in the process, finding out who she truly is. "My hope," Heather says, "is that my story and its tips will reach those who need them most. You don't need to accept adversity. You can re-write your story with the happiest of endings."

To continue with your journey towards living your best life by implementing daily rituals, visit TheHeatherWalton.com, granting you access to my free newsletter, updated content, exercises, and resources, such as **printable journal worksheets** and **a daily gratitude journal**. You can also learn about my events and services as a holistic mentor, inspirational coach, and keynote speaker.

www.ingramcontent.com/pod-product-compliance
Lightning Source LLC
Chambersburg PA
CBHW051516030726
47592CB00006B/2288